A Song of Yamhill
and Oregon's
Northwestern Willamette Valley

Gordon N. Zimmerman

Binford & Mort Publishing
Portland, Oregon

A Song of Yamhill
and Oregon's Northwestern Willamette Valley

Printed in the United States of America

Library of Congress Catalog Card Number: 2005007854

ISBN 0-8323-0560-x
ISBN 0-8323-0561-8 pbk

First Edition 2005

Table of Contents

Dedication

George S. Zimmerman
1885–1976

Mr. George S. Zimmerman was born at Yamhill, Oregon and attended local schools. He graduated from then Oregon Agricultural College, now Oregon State University, in 1910 majoring in animal husbandry. It was easy for him and his two brothers to travel to Corvallis. All Southern Pacific trains stopped in front of their house at the Kromo station. He purchased the family farm from his father in the same year. To augment his farm income, he became a livestock broker with Bodine & Clark at the Portland Oregon Stockyards. He would accumulate railroad carloads of livestock from his neighbors and ship them to the Portland stockyards. He was still listed as a broker until the yards closed.

Mr. Zimmerman's grain business operated for sixty-five years. He, or a member of his family, served on the area school boards almost continuously for sixty years. At his father's request, George Zimmerman became a secretary to a grade school board in 1907. No one else could write legible minutes of the board meetings!

Celia Dromgoole

The author also wishes to acknowledge the extraordinary historical genealogy research his sister, Celia Dromgoole, conducted. For fifty years she had filed newspaper clippings and other sources of information about the family and the Yamhill area. She has traced the history of all four grandparents. She found that there was only one Zimmerman who survived the Black Plague in Germany, one Johan Paulus Zimmerman. On the Swingle side of the family she traced back to the 1400s with Ulrick Zwingli, the noted Swiss reformer. The author did a research project in college that found that Martin Luther may have nailed his edict to the Catholic Church door, but it was Zwingli who was the true founder of the Protestant church and not Luther as many believe.

Celia traced the Swingle side of the family from Pennsylvania who came west in 1853. The William Winton Fryer family came west in 1852 from Kentucky. The author was named after Gordon Nolte, favorite brother of his Grandmother Zimmerman. Celia traced this side of the family to the great-grandfather of Nick Nolte, the movie actor.

This book is also dedicated to:

Edwin H. Enger
1913–1997

Mr. "Eddie" Enger was born at Firesteel, South Dakota. He moved with other members of his family to the Northwest in 1934. He started to work for George Zimmerman as temporary help in a prune orchard and stayed on for forty-seven years. He eventually became general manager of Zimmerman Grain Company. Eddie was involved with many other activities for many different organizations in the city of Yamhill, including being mayor and fire chief. In 1952 the author wanted to move to San Francisco to pursue music studies. Eddie urged him to go as long as he would still be listed as vice-president of Zimmerman Grain. This would aide Eddie in keeping his father in check from his overly ambitious projects that could have bankrupted the company. Eddie advised that he would look out for his interests. The plan worked and he did. In 1981 when the business was sold, enough assets were secured so that the author could retire from his job in San Francisco at the age of fifty-eight and start traveling around the world.

Christine A. Richardson-Barlow

The author also wishes to thank Christine Richardson for the many hours she has spent over many weeks and months editing and arranging the book. This put the material into a condition that would be presentable to a publishing company. It is only fitting that she and her family live in the second oldest home in Yamhill, the Lee Laughlin House.

Foreword

Just as all politics is said to be ultimately local, so can all historical studies be said to be local. Local history is the basic building block of most genres of history. This is especially true when we consider the suburban areas of large population centers. The history of Portland, and of Oregon, is made up in part of the history of the counties surrounding the metropolitan core. At present, one of these counties, Yamhill, is the outer edge of Portland's urban growth boundary. Developers look to local communities for opportunities to build homes and shopping malls, while many local residents fear the loss of their unique local cultures.

In this context, Yamhill county, and especially the town of Yamhill (pop. 970), seems sleepy, unspoiled; more remarkable for it potential than for its past. Yet within the memory of living residents, Yamhill was linked to the coastal shipping routes and to Portland by a railway system and excellent, reliable, public transportation. Today the county is not even linked by regular bus transportation.

The story of Yamhill County could not be told by a stronger more remarkable voice than that of Gordon Zimmerman. The descendant of two of the founding families, today Gordon has a foot in two worlds: he lives part of the year on a Century Farm purchased by his great-grandfather in 1863, and part of the year in a Victorian "painted lady" in San Francisco. Gordon began as his father's assistant in the feed store and became a well-known classical music singer. Today he enjoys traveling with the Friends of the 4449, a group that maintains and operates Portland's famous steam engine.

Gordon's story of Yamhill from its frontier beginnings to its current troubled place between the wild coastal range and the edges of the Portland growth boundary embraces more than a century of history. Gordon's family was in a remarkable spot from which to view not only the initial developments of the country, but also the terrible impact of the depression. Gordon ably weaves together social, economic, and cultural history. The remarkable citizens of the remote and recent pasts come alive in his narrative. He was also fortunate that his sister, Mrs. Celia Dromgoole, was a collector of early photographs of the Yamhill area.

Gordon was ably assisted in this project by another native Oregonian, Christine Richardson, co-author of the history of the Chinese in Eastern Oregon, *China Doctor of John Day*. Christine lives in Yamhill and, like Gordon, knows many of the descendants of the founders of the couny and of the city. No one is better qualified to assist Gordon in telling this remarkable story. Both Gordon and Christine are also pleased that this story can be published by Oregon's oldest press, Binford & Mort.

Jeffrey Barlow
Professor of History
Pacific University

Acknowledgements

These people encouraged me to get this book finished and supplied me with information, secured pictures and helped me in many ways during this project.

George Abdill, Debbie Ahls, Tom Ballard, Jeff and Christine Barlow, Lois Brooks, Wally Brosamle, Harry & Twila Byrnes, Jimmy Carter, Velma Chaffee, Celia Dromgoole, Gordon Dromgoole, Edith Eckrode, Evelyn Enger, Al Haij, Pat Hefflin, Clark Johnson, George Krause, Barney Kearney, Ladis and Jane Kristof, Nicholas Kristof, George Lavacot, Diane Lett, Dan Linscheid, James Loomis, Robert Melbo, Bryce Mitchell, Eleanor Mitchell, Ray Moline, Charles O'Connor, Arlene Reimers, Robert Roe, Robert Simonson, Dante Stephenson, Grant Youngbird, Multnomah County Library, Southern Pacific Transportation Company, Tillamook County Historical Society, Washington County Historical Society and Yamhill County Historical Society.

Cover Picture
Gordon Zimmerman's Century Farm in Yamhill Oregon

This picture was taken from near the top of Alex Butte looking Northeast. The hill on the background left is Bald Peak. The red fields are blossoming crimson clover grown for seed. Charles J. Swingle built the house in the middle of 1920, replacing Alexander Fryer's former house built in 1863. This house burned in 1918 on the night of Armistice Day. The barn was also built in 1863 without the use of nails in the "hole and peg" construction style.

Introduction

Yamhill: The Name and the Place

Yamhill — Anyone who has been associated with this town for very long, or for about eighty years as the author has been, has been asked hundreds of times about the origin of the name. "Where did THAT name come from? Do you grow yams on the surrounding hills?" Actually, yams will not grow in our cool, damp climate. The town was featured as Oregon's entry into the book, *Odd & Peculiar*, by Neil H. Swanson, Jr. This book features the most unusual name of a town or village or city for each of the fifty states. However, this name is one of the more significant ones in this area from before the time that Oregon became a territory.

The best evidence available shows that Yamhill is the white man's name for the Yamhill Indians. They lived along the banks of the Yamhill River, and were of the Kalapooian Tribe. Vast numbers of arrowheads have been found along the South Fork of this river during the last fifty years. A journal from 1814 refers to "Yamhelas," 'who dwell in houses on the yellow river.' (To this day the Yamhill is a muddy river most of the year.) A journal of Jason Lee's in 1834 shows the name "Yam-il" from "Che-am-il," the Indian word for bald hills. Yet another historian has stated that "Tch-yamel-amir" was another Indian word shortened to "Yam-il" that meant bald hills.

This was a very appropriate name for the tribe. Until well into the 1850s it is known that the tribe would literally set the hills on fire. On hot windy August days they would carry lighted torches and race their horses through the area that is now North Yamhill County. This would flush out game, control the underbrush to make hunting easier the next year and expose tubers they would collect for their winter use. The Indians also knew that the grass would be better the next year. This custom was carried out to the consternation of the early settlers, as it would burn their grain fields. The settlers shared their grains with the Indians during the next winter months when many of them were almost starving. This helped all parties to reach a compromise that reduced the burns. Today there is a town, a county, two rivers, and a main street in downtown Portland all named Yamhill. Yamhill Street carries part of Portland's new 44-mile light rail line west from downtown to within twenty miles of Yamhill. It has recently been announced that the Intel Corporation has a new top secret computer chip under development, code-named "Yamhill." It appears that this name is being used with increasing frequency in this ever-changing world.

The placement of the town of Yamhill was purposeful. It was on the early road from Forest Grove to Lafayette in the 1850s. The headwaters of a navigable river were at Lafayette Falls. At one time the old road was almost a straight line from Yamhill to Lafayette, a distance of only six miles. Another factor in placing the town at this site is that the early settlers would have found there was water only a few feet below the surface. In fact, during June 2004, while reconstructing Highway 47 through town on Maple Street, old gas tanks were found under sidewalks. The next morning after the tanks had been removed, clear water was standing in each of the four holes just four feet below the surface of the street. It was advised many years ago that most of the old houses of Yamhill had wells in their basements as does the Lee Laughlin house across from the grade school and the kitchen well of Alexander Fryer's house that burned in 1918 which is still under the replacement home that the author now occupies on his century farm. These often overflow after a prolonged rain when the water table rises to the surface. This is one of the reasons that the building of roads in this area has always been such a challenge.

For a number of years, many friends and relatives have requested that he must write a history of the Yamhill area. They realized, before he became aware of the fact, that he probably had a better insight into early Yamhill than almost anyone else now living in the area. Some have even been requesting that he should quit traveling all over the world for a year and get busy writing. Another friend advised, "You get busy putting your remembrances on paper now! If you don't have this started before you die, I will never speak to you again!" Finally, he realized that, yes, he does have a unique background. His family has had their roots in Yamhill for five generations. He is one of the few people in the state of Oregon that now own two Century Farms that have been continuously farmed for over 100 years by members of his family. His grandfather, Christian Zimmerman, arrived in 1883, after having spent years gold mining in Helena, Montana, where he was a partner of fabled Thomas Cruise in 1860s, and logging near Seattle. One hundred and sixteen years ago, he purchased J. J. Burton's Donation Land Claim from his heirs two miles north of Yamhill. His great, great-grandfather, Alexander Fryer, took up a Donation Land Claim in 1852 along with his brothers and father, just east of Wapato Lake. In just eleven years, he had sold it and was starting to farm two Donation Land Claims, all the land from the south edge of Yamhill for two miles to now appropriately named Fryer Road. This was quite an accomplishment, considering all the farming was done with horses and there were few roads that could be used to market products from the farm. His father, George Zimmerman, his grandfather and grandmother Swingle all had a very good sense of history. His grandmother was Alexander Fryer's daughter. Every New Year's Day, there was a reunion of all of her brothers and sisters and their families. Because his father and grandparents had been sharing stories of early day hardships, he was interested in the stories his uncles and aunts were telling in the after dinner hours and he fondly remembers these occasions throughout all of his grade and high school years. He found at an early age, that if you express interest in what older people are saying, they will go out of their way to tell you about the "Old Times," something most young people today haven't the inclination or time to get involved in.

Even though he lived in San Francisco for many years, he was still vice-president of Zimmerman Grain Company; thus necessitating his returning to Yamhill at least once or twice a year. As the years went by, whenever he would be home, his father related stories about the early Yamhill area as they drove about the countryside. He gave the history of every farm passed and every road traveled.

A Song of Yamhill is a very condensed history of the Northwest. He has used the town of Yamhill and Yamhill County in a broad sense, representing any area in the country that is now a prime agricultural area, potentially threatened by the spread of all of our cities onto this prime type of land. He has pointed out the development of roads and railroads and how geography influenced their development.

He has related the hardships of settlers in our valley. With the arrival of Ewing Young into the Chehalem Valley, just six miles east of Yamhill, he has pointed out how he saved all of the Oregon Country for the United States.

From the time of the forming of the first provincial government in the Oregon Territory forward, he stressed mainly the hardships of getting around in this area that is so rainy and wet. He pointed out how it seldom freezes, and the early pioneers were faced with a sea of mud for about eight months of the year. He outlined the development of roads, railroads and the town and County of Yamhill as an example of an early trading area.

A theme of the book is the development of the many agricultural crops in this area of a great variety of soil types. The entire county is now threatened by urban development within just a few years. At the end of the book he will point out how urban sprawl can return Yamhill to the immobility known by the early pioneers for eight months a year. The pioneers of Oregon called their problem mud. Within a few short years, if there is not a massive change in our transportation system, the same immobility will surround Yamhill. People will then call this new debilitating immobility, GRIDLOCK.

Chapter 1

Five Generations of Yamhill County Ancestors

Gordon N. Zimmerman was born August 10, 1923, the youngest child of George S. and Oka Zimmerman. He attended schools in Yamhill, graduating from high school in 1941 and from Oregon State University in June of 1949 at the time called Oregon State College. He is from a fifth generation of Yamhill residents on his mother's side of the family and from a third generation on his father's side.

While he was in college he studied Business Administration and Farm Crops. While in college he was also tenor soloist with all of the college's choral groups. On the side, he studied voice with the head of the Music Department, Paul Petrie.

When he graduated from college he had the honor of singing at the college graduation ceremonies. At that time this honor was given every year to the graduating senior who was voted by the faculty as having contributed the most to performing music during his college career. Gordon had been requested to sing at many college functions by the college president, A. L. Strand, including some events where the current state governor was in attendance. The receipt of this honor gave Gordon the courage to continue his music studies after graduation.

For the first two years after graduation, he worked at Zimmerman Grain in Yamhill. He then moved to Portland where he studied voice with Ruth Evelyn Stoughton and every summer studied with her vacationing house guest, the then well known, Florence Nydlinger of Oberlin College in Ohio. Gordon always felt she opened more doors for him vocally than any other teacher.

Oregon State News Bureau Photo

Gordon Zimmerman about to sing at graduation services at Oregon State College (now university) in June 1949. Dr. A. L. Strand, college president, is third person in the front row. He had often called on Gordon to sing at special functions.

Edris Morrison Photo

This photo of Gordon Zimmerman was used many times during the 1950s for press releases for programs on which he was a soloist.

During his time in Portland, he was a soloist with the Civic Light Opera, the Symphonic Choir, and performed in the Holiday Bowl before it became the Lloyd Shopping Center. In 1953 Gordon moved to San Francisco where he continued his studies with Gertrude Guenberg. She was a very good childhood friend of Isaac Stern, whom Gordon met on many occasions in her home.

For the next eight years he was tenor soloist with every major musical group in the San Francisco Bay area. One of his more interesting performances was as a soloist with Arthur Fiedler and the San Francisco Symphony Orchestra. He also performed with this orchestra as the tenor soloist in the United States premiere of Carl Orff's very difficult "Carmina Burana" in the San Francisco Opera House. The national music magazines gave him very favorable reviews.

During the remainder of the 1950s he concentrated on opera in concert and oratorios such as the "Elijah" and Hayden's "Creation." He performed in many requiems, including the solos for Mozart, Brahams, Schubert, Berlioz, and his favorite, the Verdi Requiem. If he did not do Handel's "Messiah" at least two times every Christmas with some group in the Bay area, he thought he was slipping!

Ken Glaser, Jr. Photo

Gordon Zimmerman can be seen coming down the steps of his home in San Francisco that he purchased in 1958 and where he still spends part of each year.

By 1960 Gordon started to have breathing and throat problems. This and Bell's Palsy that paralyzed his right face muscles, attributed to mumps, plus a new job with lots of responsibilities kept him from singing. It was not until 1978 when his doctor retired that his new doctor realized that he was a severe asthmatic and probably had been for over twenty years. His asthmatic condition was hidden from earlier detection because of his inordinately large lungs. It had always taken two x-rays to get a picture of his lungs. As a result he had been given the wrong medication for over two decades.

Gordon retired from his job in San Francisco in 1981 at an industrial insulation company. This company, MacArthur Company is the company founded by John D. and Catherine T. MacArthur of PBS sponsorship fame.

Since his retirement, Gordon has done extensive travel. Beginning in 1984 he has helped to sell souvenirs with the *4449* Steam Engine Support Group that was formed to maintain the steam engine used in the 1976 United States tour of the Freedom Train. He has been on every trip of that group since then. Gordon has sold souvenirs on these trips and with his powerful speaking voice has been very helpful on these trips. He also coordinated selling souve-

Gordon Zimmerman Collection
The author has been on many special trains, mainly selling souvenirs on *4449* steam excursions. Here, he is part of the staff on a special Union Pacific Railroad train operating from Denver to Portland.

Gordon Zimmerman Photo

Periodically the *4449* is used on trips from Portland to Bend. Above, it is crossing a trestle near Madras. Mt. Jefferson is to the right.

Harvey Rosener Photo

The *4449* concession car owned by *Friends of 4449*. Left to right: George Lavacot, Gary Oslund, Bill Slover, Pat Tracey, Gordon Zimmerman, and Doyle McCormack locomotive engineer. All of the above have been members of the *4449* crew since at least 1984.

nirs between trips to keep them available on demand. This group recently bestowed on him the honor of naming their Souvenir Sales Car "Gordon N. Zimmerman," formerly a baggage car used on the Union Pacific Streamliner Passenger Train Fleet. This honor is usually bestowed posthumously.

Mr. Zimmerman has traveled extensively by rail on a number of continents. In Europe and Australia he rode rails that were identical and built at the same time as those once operated in the United States during the 1920s. Some of his most enjoyable travels to very remote and scenic places have been with the High Iron Travel's special using the four cars shown in the photo on page 50. This includes a trip to Great Slave Lake in the Northwest Territories, the northern most point reached by rail on the North American continent. He has also traveled over most lines in Mexico on these cars, where he crossed over into Guatemala. On another very memorable trip he used these cars on a special train to Plains, Georgia, where our train was met by former president, Jimmy Carter, who was on the station platform. Later, at a barbecue honoring our group that evening, Carter sat across from the author. Introducing himself as being from Yamhill, Oregon, the author told of reading in the local papers that Carter had taken a fishing

Dante Stephensen Photo
The author and former president Jimmy Carter at a BBQ honoring the American Association of Private Railway Car Owners in Plains, Georgia.

During May 1989, the *4449* traveled to Los Angeles for the 50th anniversary of Union Station. More souvenirs were sold than on any other trip up to this time. To honor Gordon, he was made the fireman from Eugene for a much-publicized entry into Portland. A regular fireman that helped him pull all the right levers was Pat Tracy, standing in the doorway.

trip to the upper reaches of the Nestucca River. Carter advised that this had been one of his more memorable fishing trips, recalling that he had caught three large steelhead in one hour and Rosalyn caught two as well. Another trip on these cars was when they were included in a 21-car American Association of Private Railroad Car Owners special train from Chicago to Hoboken, New Jersey using only freight lines along the way. As on other trips everyone slept on the train at our terminal point. These self-contained cars have dining, lounge, sleeping, and all cars have showers. Collectively, this train is valued at over $15 million. Right before we returned west, a banquet was held for us on the 102nd floor of the World Trade Center. After the banquet and meeting, a fireworks display was held for us, shot from a barge nearby in the Hudson River. The display was given to the group by one of the car owners. In light of 9-11, it was an experience he will always remember looking down on the fireworks from that place that no longer exists.

His paternal grandfather was Christian Zimmerman born in 1848 in Siberingville, Ontario near Toronto, Canada. He eventually traveled west three times before he brought his bride to Yamhill, Oregon. On his first trip west he traveled south to St. Louis and then traveled by riverboat to the headwaters of navigation on the Missouri River at Fort Benton, Montana. He was only fifteen years old.

He then traveled on to Helena on foot. He was an early partner of Thomas Cruise of that city. He traveled on to the Fraser River country where he was also moderately successful at mining. From Vancouver he traveled south and crossed the Isthmus on the Panama Railroad and then by riverboat up the Mississippi and eventually into Canada.

Christian Zimmerman soon traveled west again and established logging and fishing operations on Whidby and Vashon Islands. The Census of June 12, 1880 shows that he operated a logging camp of ten white men and one Chinese cook, Ah Foo.

Celia Dromgoole Collection

Christian Zimmerman would take his horses, normally used in logging, to a beach where they would be attached to a fishing boat's net. The boat would sail off shore and the horses would pull the other end of the net up the beach. When the net was full the horses would pull it and its contents ashore.

By 1882 he had sold this logging operation and land at 5th and Bell streets in downtown Seattle and returned to Siberingville where he married his childhood sweetheart, Louisa Nolte. Her youngest brother became the great-grandfather of Nick Nolte, the movie actor.

Before he left the West, he arranged to purchase a portion of John J. Burton's Donation Land Claim two miles north of present day Yamhill, Oregon. Christian Zimmerman eventually acquired several thousand acres in this area before his death in 1934.

In the spring of 1883, he traveled west again on a most unique travel conveyance on the Northern Pacific Railroad and the C. B. & Q (Chicago, Burlington, & Quincy). The lines had started to run immigrant trains from Chicago to St. Paul to Portland, Oregon. As soon as the new Northern Pacific Line opened in 1882, they charged only one dollar for a family to go west in a special boxcar that had water tanks overhead. The family's animals were stabled in one end

God Bless Our Home.

Residence of Mr. *C Zimmerman* — Town of *Northyamhill* — State of Oregon.
On the Line of the OREGON PACIFIC RAILROAD.

Celia Dromgoole Collection

Christian Zimmerman house about 1885 – OPRR was sixty miles south at Corvallis. Railroad photographers would take pictures of large buildings on connecting railroads and claim them for their advertising books. George Zimmerman is the smaller standing boy, second from right.

Celia Dromgoole Collection
Christian Zimmerman sold the south end of his farm to his son George, in 1910. This is the new home Christian built on the north end of his land. Christian and Louisa's son Edward, is with them in this photo.

Celia Dromgoole Collection
The Zimmermans about 1912. Rear: George, Peter, Frank. Front Row: Christian, Edward, Louisa. One of these men was on a school board in Yamhill or Cove Orchard almost continuously from 1892 until the 1960s.

Celia Dromgoole Collection
This is the Wesleyan Church built by Christian Zimmerman, at Main & Fir Sts. This building became the west wing of the Christian Church.

of the car, their farming implements were placed in the other end, and their furniture, beds, and tables, etc. were placed in the center of the car for use. Coal stoves for cooking were also installed in these special boxcars. Straw, hay, and water were provided at division stops along the way. The car was stopped right at the Zimmerman farm at Krono for off loading. Try that for service today!

The family of Gordon Zimmerman's mother has been in the Yamhill area for five generations. His grandparents took up some of the first Donation Land Claims in Carlton and the very north edge of Yamhill County.

The first grandfather (great, great-grandfather) was Peter Chimicum Smith. He was born in 1792 in Lincoln County, North Carolina. His solitary grave is on Main Street on the west edge of Carlton. The site was a former Methodist Church, now a private home.

Mr. Smith's first wife died in 1831 in Illinois leaving him with five children. He remarried. By 1844, when he was 52, he set out for Oregon with second wife, Ortha Dean, two very small children, three children from his first marriage, and a son-in-law. He traveled the Oregon Trail, the first of three of Zimmerman's grandfathers to

W. C. Little Photo, Celia Dromgoole Collection

F. C. Graham purchased several hundred acres three miles north of Yamhill during 1910. He founded Cove Orchard. Note the railroad across the middle of the picture.

Celia Dromgoole Collection

Note the church in the above picture of Cove Orchard. It was the Presbyterian Church one-half mile from C. Zimmerman's new 1910 home. His wife is eighth from the left. This is the third church they helped build in the area.

travel that route, about which has been said that the brave started it and only the strong survived it. This great hardship of going west from the Mississippi Basin was justified because the Midwest was growing many more crops than could be used locally or could be shipped down that river to New Orleans for a new market there. Even exporting the over-produced crops proved problematic.

Mr. Smith took out a Donation Land Claim for 643.15 acres Certificate No. 121, dated April 17, 1845. This is the ground on which the city of Carlton is now located. He built a house and a red barn on what is now Park and Polk streets. The barn still stands and over the years has been used as a rose nursery.

Mr. Smith was a blacksmith and a farmer. He gave the land and most of the money to build a Methodist Church. His burial site that now has a white picket fence surrounding the grave is on this site. It is reported that he was the lay minister for the church and also a teacher in the local school. The headstone reads:

Peter Smith
Died June 5, 1863
71 yrs, 3 mos, & 4 ds
"Remember man as you pass by
As you are so once was I.
As I am now so must you be
Prepare for death and follow me."

In later years his wife, Ortha Dean, lived with her daughter, Elizabeth, the wife of Alexander Fryer. In 1900 she took a train and boat to Bandon, Oregon and on to Coquille. She had two brothers in that area, one of them the editor of the local newspaper. She had traveled there to care for triplets just born to a granddaughter. At eighty-eight years old she complained in her last letter to her daughter that it was heavy packing two five gallon pails of water up the hill from a creek below. She died before she could return to Yamhill. Records are still being searched for her actual gravesite.

Mr. Zimmerman's other great, great-grandfather was William Winton Fryer who was born in 1798 in Prince William County, Virginia. He moved to Greene County, Kentucky and married Sarah Vaughn who was born in 1796 in Tennessee. By 1852 they sold their land in Greene County and with their children left Kentucky with 275 horses to travel west on the Oregon Trail to the Oregon Territory. They had sold all their property and had freed all their

Celia Dromgoole Collection

This home was built in 1863 by Alexander Fryer. It was built in a style typical of homes in Kentucky. It burned Nov. 11, 1918. It was replaced by the home shown on the cover.

Celia Dromgoole Collection

Alexander Fryer at age 89 in front of T & E store. This photograph was taken in 1918.

slaves. They had been advised that the U.S. Army would buy all of the Kentucky horses that could be brought west.

This type of horse bred with Indian ponies would produce the kind of horse that the army needed at that time in Oregon Country.

Coming west, the Fryer men only lost about sixty horses to the Indians. In the Great Salt Lake region, according to family lore, gangs of Mormons chased off eighty horses under cover of night. However, when the Fryers got to what is now Laurelwood, Oregon, the most severe freeze on record ensued. They had arrived too late to build shelter but were told not to worry as it never freezes in Oregon. Unfortunately, that winter it got down to almost zero for days on end and all but thirty-five of their horses froze to death. Zimmerman's grandmother often said her father had advised that one of the most awful periods of his life was listening to the braying of the horses day and night as they were freezing to death. To keep the wind off, they had driven the horses up a draw but to no effect. It is all the more remarkable that the family went on to be so successful. All of the Fryer men took homesteads east of Gaston on the Yamhill, Washington county line. They took Donation Land Claims, Certificate No. 4564 and Certificate No. 8072.

These men were very successful in their coming generations. In just eleven years the senior Mr. Fryer died and all of their Gaston holdings were sold in 1863. With the proceeds Alexander Fryer purchased about 400 acres south of Yamhill on the Yamhill-Lafayette Road. His brother, John T., purchased about 400 acres a mile further south on this road. Earlier, James M. had bought out his employer, Mr. Stillwell, to run the general store in Yamhill. In nine years he opened a store at First and Madison streets in Portland. Within a few years the younger brother, Flavious, opened the first store in Carlton just three miles south of Yamhill. In spite of the huge loss of their horses in the winter of 1852 they were a most industrious and successful family.

Gordon Zimmerman's maternal grandmother was Orpha Fryer, a daughter of Alexander. She and her only daughter, his mother, met their husbands in a most interesting and coincidental manner, explained later in this narrative.

Zimmerman's great-grandfather, Joseph Swingle, was born in 1819 in Pennsylvania, neighbors to Joseph Smith, who eventually founded the Church of Latter Day Saints, often called the Mormon Church. He came west more than once like Christian Zimmerman. His first trip's destination was near Oakland, California during the

Celia Dromgoole Collection

The author's great-grandfather, Joseph Conrad Swingle, 1819-1896. He arrived in Medford in 1853. He took up a homestead, built a number of sawmills in the area and took up a second homestead with his children in Klamath County.

Celia Dromgoole Collection

Joseph Swingle built this house in 1872 in Langell Valley. It was later purchased by his son Charles. The last Indian uprising in the U.S. took place on this ranch in 1872.

Gold Rush. He soon sold out and returned to his home in Wisconsin and married in 1841. In 1853 he became the captain of a wagon train and brought his wife and friends over the Applegate Trail to Antelope Creek near Medford. In 1866 Zimmerman's grandfather, Charles Swingle, was born on that farm where, in 1872, his mother died. The family moved to the south end of Langell Valley, east of Klamath Falls, where they all filed for adjoining homesteads on February 28, 1883. They paid Simpson Wilson $1.50 a day to build their houses.

Within a short time after the Swingles and a number of other settlers had taken over the land, Indian leader, Captain Jack, began to cause trouble. The U.S. Army was in the area and Captain Jack and his followers were finally captured in the Stronghold area in northern California. This was the last Indian uprising in the U.S. and it had started on the Swingle's land holdings! Coincidentally in 1856 Alexander Fryer and all of his brothers were enlisted into the Army to fight in the Indian wars in northwest Oregon. They were inducted on January 28, 1856 in Company C, 2nd Battalion, 1st Regiment, OMV-Portland. On April 13, 1856 they were mustered out.

Eventually Gordon's grandfather purchased his brother Oliver's and his father's holdings. Over the years he purchased adjoining ranches until his ranch totaled about 2000 acres.

Celia Dromgoole Collection
Charles Swingle beside his 1920s Buick. The running board was a handy place to transport a just dressed out calf to a local market.

Hay being pulled into a barn at Swingle Ranch in southern Klamath County
in the 1920s. This scene was repeated in most barns throughout the Willamette
Valley.

This valley now known for its great fields of alfalfa for hay
had no irrigation in the 1880s. The Swingles were in need of alfalfa
hay to augment their grass hay. Here begins a most amazing tale of
his two families. As Ruth Stoller of the Yamhill County Historical
Society once advised our forefathers went to great hardships to get
around. This family first hooked up all their hay wagons and horses
and drove them over 106 miles to Ashland over Green Springs Mountain. Here they put their horses in a livery stable for care while they
were gone. Then they took a train to Yamhill to buy a carload or two
of alfalfa hay. Frank Swingle knew Dolly Mesner who lived west of
Yamhill. The Mesners did not have enough alfalfa hay. Since the
Mesners knew the Swingles were coming to buy alfalfa, they arranged
for them to buy alfalfa from Alexander Fryer who had a railroad
siding on his property. It's not to worry about Frank, he married
Dolly Mesner within a few years.

Every year for many years the Swingles repeated the journey
each June to buy alfalfa hay. Within a few years Charles was making
eyes at Alexander Fryer's daughter, Orpha. They eventually married in 1890.

Gordon Zimmerman Collection

Christian Zimmerman sold this home to his son, George, the author's father, during 1910. Left-hand portion was built in 1883. The balance was built during the 1890s. The house burned in 1950.

Gordon Zimmerman Photo

The author's grandfather, Charles Swingle, built this house in downtown Klamath Falls for weekend and winter use so that his daughter could go to high school across the street. Gordon, at age fifteen, and his grandmother Orpha Swingle on the steps.

For the next eighteen years the Swingles were still hauling hay every June. This became a time for the three families, the Swingles, Fryers and the Mesners, to have a reunion in Yamhill. During one year Alexander Fryer did not have enough hay and he arranged for the Swingles to purchase more alfalfa hay from Christian Zimmerman two miles north of Yamhill. In the year 1908 Mr. Zimmerman's father, George Zimmerman, started making eyes at the Swingle's only daughter, Oka. History repeated itself, they were married January 1, 1911 at the Klamath Falls home of the Swingles. For years they had maintained a second home in downtown Klamath Falls. By this time the Gerber Reservoir had been built and irrigation water was now available in Langell Valley, resulting in lots of alfalfa hay in that valley. Gordon's grandfather Swingle was president of the Irrigation District for years. The area is still known for its superior alfalfa hay.

Charles Swingle purchased Alexander Fryer's family home in 1918 and built the present house during 1920. He planted eighty acres of prunes, built a large prune dryer, and built the century farm home, now Mr. Zimmerman's residence. Charles sold his stock ranch in Langell Valley in 1937 and moved permanently to Yamhill. Mr. Zimmerman can justly be proud of his parents and grandparents' perseverance and very hard work in pioneering the Yamhill area.

Chapter 2

Oregon Territory and Yamhill Secured for the United States

Before 1840, when the streams of covered wagons started to roll toward the Oregon Country, there were four groups of white settlers within just a few miles of Yamhill. They all had the same desire to find a rich, virgin peaceful land where they might settle and prosper.

The largest group was Hudson's Bay Company employees at Fort Vancouver. Fort Vancouver was located on the north bank of the Columbia River, near the mouth of the Willamette River. The line between the British Government and the Hudson's Bay Company was murky; something like the former line between the Russian Government and the Communist Party.

The next group of people were former French-Canadian fur trappers that had settled in a colony about eighteen miles east of Yamhill. They had grown old in Hudson's Bay Company's service; many had settled down and taken Indian wives. This group of farmers really had it good. The company was their patron, everything they needed was provided. They had fixed prices for all their needs, plus social security and paid up medical care. They were very much beholden to the head of the Hudson's Bay Company, Dr. John McLoughlin.

The third group has been more widely publicized than any other. These were the missionaries of what would become Yamhill and adjoining Marion Counties. The most famous was Jason Lee. He was dedicated but impractical. He dreamed of converting the Indians, mixing them into the white race and then have everybody march along with him singing hymns to God and a great and prosperous Oregon. What he failed to see at that time was that it would take generations to reach this utopia and it might not be desirous or possible.

Jason Lee gathered around him a large group of fellow missionaries. Most had impractical dreams. By 1850, a system of circuit riders was established with ministers preaching in each settlement throughout the Willamette Valley about once every six weeks; lay people kept the church together between visits. All of the services were held in people's homes. Various churches in the eastern United States supported these frontier missions to the 'Wild West'. Every little hamlet in New England and the rest of the East held bazaars, pie socials and quilting bees to support their churches' frontier missions. It is believed that the very first mission to be established in the area was an Episcopal Indian mission established in 1842 five miles northwest of Yamhill. It was run by Bishop Richmond for whom Mt. Richmond is now named. They secured a section of land, built a log cabin and started a school for Indian children. The loss of their daughter who died and discouragement at the lack of results in their efforts to teach the Indians, caused the Richmonds to return to their home in Rhode Island in 1852. However, there have been positive results from the operation of Indian schools. Today, there is a young lady who works in Yamhill whose great, great grandmother attended a similar school. Her family history advises that these schools had a positive effect on the students in teaching them marketable skills.

A Methodist Church was founded in Yamhill in 1849, the same year a Methodist Church was founded in Lafayette and Oregon City. These three were the first Methodist churches in Oregon.

Dr. McLoughlin looked upon the missionaries with the greatest of approval. He gave them goods, services and a few family cattle. Outside of Vancouver in 1840 there were nearly as many ministers in Oregon as there were all other white men. It must be remembered that the French trappers and the missionaries were deeply indebted to the kindly Dr. McLoughlin. What happened in just a few short years upon the death of Ewing Young is all the more remarkable.

The fourth group of white settlers arriving before 1840 had more influence in securing the Oregon Territory for the United States than all the other groups combined. Ewing Young led a contrasting group to the Oregon Territory. He was a young man, so outstanding that leadership fell naturally to him. Nobody paid him to come to Oregon; as was the case with the missionaries and the trappers.

Manhood came early to Young in Eastern Tennessee. He soon found himself leading large groups of men on tough trapping expeditions in Mexico. Over the next several years they worked their way north and west, through New Mexico, Arizona and California. His companions were such men as Kit Carson and his cousin, Alex (sometimes spelled "Alec," but most references are spelled "Alex"). Ewing Young's word was accepted by merchants, trappers, Indians, and Spanish Officials. In short, he was a man of great skill and daring.

Shortly after his group arrived in San Diego; Young met Hall J. Kelly, Oregon's most dedicated publicist. Kelly advised him that Oregon was destined to become the fairest part of the United States. As a man who had endured great thirst, poisoned waters and incredible heat in the Southwest, Young was now at a crossroads. He had accumulated nothing. The promise of free land with lots of water in a mild climate made him realize he should settle down. He had seen great vistas and had accomplished much. Young still had his great strength and endurance. He gathered a group of ten of his men and a hundred horses and rode to Oregon from San Diego.

Then ensued a very strange encounter. Governor Figueroa of the San Francisco area did not know Young and he erroneously jumped to the conclusion that Young was the leader of a gang of horse thieves. He wrote to Dr. McLoughlin and Jason Lee. Together they agreed to boycott Young and drive him from the territory. They put out an order that all who dealt with him would be boycotted.

Young's party arrived in 1834 and settled in the Chehalem Valley, just seven miles east of Yamhill. His heart was full of hope and kindness. He was soon flabbergasted to learn that he could not buy a pound of salt or coffee, nor could he trade horses for one or two cows. He knew he had done nothing wrong.

As his grain crops grew and accumulated, because of McLoughlin and Lee, he did what he had to do to survive. He found cauldrons, pipes and other machinery from an abandoned trading post on Sauvies Island at the mouth of the Willamette River. McLoughlin had put this post out of business a few years before. He put them on small boats and paddled them up the Willamette and Yamhill Rivers to Lafayette where it was only six miles over level ground to his holdings. Young then proceeded to set up a small distillery; after all he grew up in Tennessee. He sold liquor to Indians and Whites. It worked; he survived. In the last twenty years a very large number of bottles suitable for liquer were unearthed at his homesite.

Destiny took a hand. In late 1836, President Andrew Jackson decided to find out what was going on out in far off Oregon. He sent William A. Slocum as his personal ambassador.

Slocum soon sailed up the Columbia River to Fort Vancouver. An alarmed Dr. McLoughlin wined and dined him like a king. What was up? Slocum carried no cargo and there were no plans for trade. Soon, Slocum became alarmed by the feudal ways of the Hudson's Bay Company with all the settlers under thralldom to Dr. McLoughlin.

Slocom proceeded to French Prairie where he found huge crops of wheat growing near the Willamette River. He then proceeded to Lee's Mission Bottom farm where he found crops producing every type of agricultural need for the settlers and their animals.

Slocum had heard about Ewing Young's distillery. He traveled to see Young and finally heard his side of what was really going on in Oregon. It is reported that there was an instant liking between the two men.

It became clear to Slocum what must be done and it must be done fast if the Oregon Territory was to be saved for the United States:

> Arouse a community spirit among the American settler as distinct from the British.
> Have Young dismantle his distillery.
> Overcome the anti-Young sentiment.
> Break the complete stranglehold of the Hudson's Bay Company. The Company owned all the cattle. They only loaned some to each settler, but would sell none and the company took the increase each year.

A meeting was called for January 13, 1837. With Slocum's encouragement, Young agreed to dismantle the distillery. This dispelled the ill feeling against Young. Slocum then formed the Willamette Valley Cattle Company and made Young it's head. He arranged for financing and sent Young to California to buy cattle.

Remarkably, Young was successful in dealing with Mexican California for the cattle. After all, just a few years prior to this trading mission, the Mexican Governor had thought Young to be a horse thief. Additionally, California had a policy of not exporting any cattle. However, Young was able to purchase 800 head and returned with 630 still alive. He sold them to any and all settlers for $7.30 each — free and clear. Young even gave credit.

Slocum's objectives were accomplished. Americans began working together and no longer looked to Hudson's Bay Company for leadership. It was at this point, that the complete domination by McLoughlin of the Oregon Country was broken.

W.D. Warmington Photo
Schools of Old Yamhill *by Ruth Stoller, Yamhill County Historical Society*

Zimmerman School was organized in 1892 on the north edge of Zimmerman farm. In 1916, it was replaced by a new school in Cove Orchard one half-mile north. George Zimmerman moved the building to the northwest corner of his home where it was used as a woodshed. Yes, willow switches were used on the author in this building.

Young prospered. He built a sawmill and established a trading post. Young dealt with fairness and soon became the bank for the Americans. When he died in 1841 without heirs, it became apparent that a provisional government would have to be set up to settle his considerable estate. This led to the now famous meeting at Champoeg. In 1843 the white settlers met to determine if Oregon should be American or British. A line was drawn on the ground, those in favor of the United States on one side, the ones in favor of Great Britain on the other. A late arriving American settler, Joe Meek arrived just in time to stand on the American side of the line, breaking the tie, according to what I've read.

It was a close call for the Americans. One must remember that Dr. McLoughlin had most of the French-Canadians, and missionaries and many of the American settlers indebted to him. If

Ewing Young had not rebelled at the benevolent dictatorship of the Hudson's Bay Company and defied McLoughlin; if William Slocum had not re-installed him in the eyes of the settlers; if Young's first cattle importation plan had not succeeded, then Oregon might never have become a part of the United States.

This was the beginning of the end of the Hudson's Bay Company. Since 1825, Dr. McLoughlin had made huge profits for the British, whose government he represented. Trapping was declining. By the late 1840s he left the Company, became a U.S. Citizen, took a homestead at Oregon City and opened a store. He continued to help settlers from the Oregon Trail. He became hated and in later years much loved by settlers arriving on the Oregon Trail. His Oregon City home is now a National Park Service Historic Site.

Five years after Ewing Young's death, an oak tree was planted in the soil of his grave. It is located just south of his trading post and home on Chehalem Creek. The now large oak tree can be seen today at the north end of a lane at 18715 NE Hwy 240, about seven miles east of Yamhill.

Photo courtesy of Oregon Travel Information Council
This oak tree, east of Yamhill on Highway 240, marks the grave of Ewing Young, whose death led to the formation of the Provisional Government of Oregon in 1843.

Chapter 3

The Beginning of Yamhill County

The new provisional government at Champoeg divided the Oregon Country into four districts. There were no white settlers in Washington or Eastern Oregon. The first district was called Tuality — all lands south of the yet to be determined Canadian border and west of the Willamette River and to the South to the Chehalem and Parrot Mountains, (these mountains are located in the north part of the Willamette Valley).

The second district was called Yamhill. It contained all lands south of Tuality and west of the Willamette River and on a line straight on south to California. The only north — south pass through these 1000 foot high mountains were just three miles north of the soon to be established town of Yamhill.

Champoeg District was everything north and east to the Rocky Mountains. Clackamas was everything else east to the Rocky Mountains.

This was a vast area. Beginning in 1843 it had a framework of government. The stage was now set to receive travelers via the Oregon Trail from all parts of the United States.

One of the first acts of the new provisional government was to require all male citizens perform at least one day of road work each year. However, the early pioneers were a hardy, yet independent lot. This ruling was so unpopular that it was abolished by 1848.

The Homestead and Donation Land Claim Acts were established by Congress in 1850. Getting around in the vast area of Champoeg and Clackamas in the 1840s and 1850s was very simple, you walked. If you were lucky, you had a horse to ride. Boats on the Willamette and Yamhill Rivers only served a relatively small area.

One of the most remarkable cases of "getting around" occurred in the late 1830s. The ill-fated Astor expedition at Astoria was sold to the British along with all of their employees. After the passage of some time, one employee, Louis La Bonte, wanted to stop trapping and start farming. McLoughlin was alarmed. La Bonte was retiring from trapping when he was at a far too young an age. McLoughlin was afraid if he allowed La Bonte to retire that other trappers would follow suit.

McLoughlin finally allowed La Bonte to resign, but he had to resign in Montreal. If he quit in Oregon, La Bonte would be subject to arrest. La Bonte bade him farewell and calmly walked to Montreal, resigned and walked back to his wife and family in Oregon, (approximately 8000 miles). One can only imagine the look on McLoughlin's face when La Bonte handed him the proper documents. La Bonte became a good friend of Ewing Young's. When the provisional government was formed La Bonte was one of the few former French trappers that voted with the Americans.

By the last half of the 1840s, the westward migration was increasing every year. The official end of the Oregon Trail was at the Oregon City Falls on the Willamette River. Here, freight was hauled and people walked around the falls. A boat could then be taken to Champoeg at the confluence of the Willamette and Yamhill Rivers. Another boat could then be taken on up the Yamhill River to the head of navigation at Yamhill Falls. These falls are located directly south of the present day Lafayette City Park, not at Yamhill Locks, which lies one mile east.

The first post office in Yamhill County was established at the falls with the name of Yam Hill Falls on January 8, 1850. This office was moved a few blocks north and renamed Lafayette on March 14, 1851. On that same date, a post office was established at North Yamhill just six miles north on the road to Tualatin Plains with Benjamin Stewart, Postmaster. This was only five years after the first U.S. mail was delivered in Oregon.

During the late 1840s, the first riverboat was established from Yam Hill Falls to Oregon City. It was a huge success. It was powered by four Indian rowers. These primitive craft were called bateaus. The charge to Oregon City was $35.00 per ton and was the first regular transportation service out of Yamhill County. However, sheep and cattle were still driven to Portland on foot.

During the 1850s a whole procession of steamboats started service from Yamhill Falls to Oregon City. Yamhill Steamboat Company was formed. But life was not a bed of roses for those on the boats. The river rose and fell. Log jams and bars were formed overnight. One never knew if you would be stuck in the middle of the river or against the bank under the trees. On top of all of this, the boats had a distressing habit of blowing up, scattering passengers and crew among the tree branches. In spite of all of this, the river was the only year-round outlet for people living west of Lafayette and on up the Willamette to Corvallis. Regularly scheduled boat traffic was offered on the Yamhill River until about 1900.

Chapter 4

Trails and Roads Started
As Oregon Becomes a Territory:
North Yamhill is Born

From the time of Ewing Young, all roads in Northwest Oregon were actually nothing more than Indian trails that the early settlers adapted for their use. On March 3, 1849, a giant step was taken when Oregon received territorial status. This came about because of the 1847 Marcus Whitman massacre in Walla Walla. The war department was now obliged to secure and defend the Oregon Territory. In 1849, five hundred dragoons and infantrymen arrived at Fort Vancouver.

In 1854, Congress authorized a military road from Astoria to Salem. In his report, Lt. George Derby stated there was no need to build a new road from Plainview at the summit of Cornelius Pass to Lafayette as a good road already existed with a boat connection from Ft. Vancouver over this pass to Lafayette and on to Salem. Lt. Derby then proceeded to build a road north from this summit following various mountain ridges all the way to Astoria. When asked by an Astorian why he routed the Astoria road across Saddle Mountain, he replied, "I went to special pains to make my road across the summit of every mountain and hill to Astoria, I could not afford to miss Saddle Mountain." This mountain was 2200 feet high. Clear up to the time of the Model T automobile it was the policy and much more practical to route a road up a mountain and along a ridge than to follow any flat land or valley. There is an extremely simple answer for this policy. It was easier to drive cattle, pull a wagon or even ride a horse up and down over dry hills than it was to take a wagon up to its hubs through the mud of the valley floors. It was bad enough crossing these valleys to get from one hill to the next. Here a corduroy road of fallen trees or planks laid across the valley

was used. Ray Moline and Tom Roe who both lived near Dewey
Corners, once advised me that the crossing of the valley by the
Yamhill to Bald Peak road near their family farms was the worst
mud hole on this entire road. This was the narrowest place to cross
Chehalem Creek. They advised that many a time they drug small
trees and planks over to this road. This was done out of self protec-
tion. Otherwise travelers would be over to their houses at all hours
of the day or night when it was most inconvenient, and request that
they harness up horses to pull them out of the mud. The trees small
enough to handle would only last a short time before they rotted out
and the whole process would have to be done all over again. In
comparison, going up and down over hills was so easy and you could
travel it for eight months a year instead of only three or four months
on other types of roads.

Except for a road or trail from the river at Lafayette, the earliest road into North Yamhill appears to have been a trail constructed
during the 1830s from Fort Vancouver to the Tualatin Plains. It would
have been an easy boat trip down the Columbia River to the shel-
tered west side of Sauvies Island to the foot of Cornelius Pass. At
579 feet above sea level, this is by far the lowest notch in all of
Portland's west hill's passes. From Tualatin Plains, the road headed
west to what is now Hillsboro, to near Dilley south of Forest Grove
and on to a rocky fjord across the Tualatin River long used by the
Indians. From here there was an old Indian trail up the north face
of Bald Peak. The ridge was followed for a few miles, then the road
proceeded down the west side to Dewey Corners. From here, the
main road followed Ribbon Ridge to east of Kuhne and Abbey Roads
to Lafayette. This is the road that Lt. Darby mentioned in his report, that went on to Salem.

It is only through references such as these that all early roads
in Yamhill County can be determined. The courthouse in Lafayette
burned in January 1857, leaving no records of any kind. All roads
were re-surveyed using dates of 1857 and 1858, as dates constructed
even though some roads were in use for years. Earlier roads can be
determined by checking dates in adjoining cemeteries, other land-
marks, and early writings.

By the 1850s, there was a two-story hotel at Dewey Corners
where a road branched southwest, crossing the valley near Ray
Moline's place near what is now Laughlin Road to North Yamhill.
For many years, this would have been the easiest road from Yamhill
to Portland.

It was not until 1856, that the Tualatin Plains Plank Road Company completed a primitive toll road out of downtown Portland up what is now Canyon Road and intersected the Cornelius Pass Road. Many miles would have been saved travelers by using this new road to downtown Portland.

Between 1849, when Oregon was proclaimed a territory, and 1859 when the State of Oregon was created and for decades later, the biggest problem facing the new government was roads and how people could move within the area. To use the word road for most of the roads built until the 1900s would be misleading to present day readers. Most started out as Indian trails. Most were re-routed and moved to hills. Many had planks or trees laid across them. Naturally, the wood was not chemically treated and lasted just two or three years. Most were not fit for wagons except for about four months in the summer, the remainder of the year they were only suitable for pack trains. Most tonnage actually moved by pack trains much of the year. Horses and mules would be mired down to their bellies and would have to be unloaded. Some would not be able to be pulled out of the muck or they would break a leg falling through broken corduroy logs; these animals would be shot on site. Ray Moline advised that he and his father used to go down to the corduroy road near their farm with a team of horses and a chain to pull out animals that had been shot, they would then drag them to their pig pen. Here the animals' bellies would be cut open with an ax. Pigs were efficient scavengers.

Many times whole wagons would be mired to their axles. One must realize that it seldom freezes in winter long enough to allow one to travel over frozen roads. Almost all movement had to be done in the short summer months. During winter months' families would be mostly isolated to small areas around their homes. This frustration is shown by the following example, as I remember this incident occurred in 1933 when I was ten years old.

My maternal grandfather, Charles Swingle, was a man who never swore or cursed. One early spring he came to Yamhill from his cattle ranch forty miles east of Klamath Falls. One day I happily went with him as he drove west of Yamhill to try to collect some money. He had a heavy 1927 four-door Buick car. On the first call he received no money, but got stuck. He got out of this mud hole by everyone at this home and myself pushing. It was here I learned to stay away from spinning rear wheels. At the second home, he got stuck again. We had to be pulled out by a team of horses this time.

Gordon Zimmerman Photo

The Bunn House, the first fine home built in North Yamhill in 1872. It was sold to John Bunn, the grandfather of Beverly Cleary, author of many children's books and the bestseller, *A Girl from Yamhill*.

Twila Byrnes Collection

This was the second fine home built in North Yamhill. It was built in 1879 by Lee Laughlin, the local banker. From left, Loleta, Mrs. Ben and Twila Reimers (Brynes). Photo taken about 1926.

On the way home, on a county road, we went through a dry looking surface crust and really got stuck. I will always remember Grandpa who never swore, bursting out, "Why can't this G— D— country freeze up in winter as in Klamath county like God intended so one can get around." His big Buick was far too heavy for roads used mainly by horses and Model T Fords. To this day, one can only travel on established graveled roads during winter months.

In spite of all of these incredible hardships, our forefathers did get around. They took out land claims, farmed the land and created families and communities.

The only record of an organization established in North Yamhill before 1851, was the Methodist Church. It was founded December 4, 1849. A Methodist Church was founded on the same date in Lafayette and in Oregon City. This was the time of the

Yamhill United Methodist Church Collection
The Methodist Church built in 1898. Christian Zimmerman always claimed that he supplied most of the funds for the building, $995.00.

circuit riders. This was the beginning of Yamhill becoming the earliest trading area for this part of the Oregon Territory.

During the mid-1850s records indicate that there was a great deal of buying and selling of land around the area six miles north of Lafayette, where four donation land claims came together. This area was to become North Yamhill. The second postmaster was William Stillwell, appointed on April 29, 1858. Records indicate that the post office was located in some sort of store. Family history advises that he was not much of a storekeeper. He claimed to have been founder of Yamhill. He soon lost interest and was never around, eventually he sold the store to his employee, James M. Fryer. Mr. Fryer had worked for Stillwell from the time he opened of the store. Records indicate Mr. Fryer was postmaster from December 14, 1860, until October 8, 1869. He was the brother of Alexander Fryer, my great-grandfather. During these ten years, the town became an active trading center. However, the spirit of the old west prevailed. The town was never plotted and recorded. It became known as the town without a proprietor. Whenever somebody needed a piece of land on which to open a business, they simply went to the current owners of the donation land claims on Maple or Olive Streets and

Gordon Zimmerman Photo
This house was built in 1872 by Alexander Fryer's brother James M. He worked for Stillwell when he opened the first store in Yamhill. James bought him out and was at the store for about fifteen years.

went shopping for the best price for a suitable piece of land. When a deal was made for a lot sufficient for the current needs, it was sliced off the corner of a donation land claim like a piece of cake and numbered by range and township. Some of these odd size lots are still on the records today, such as 18' x 100', 36' x 105', 23' x 100', etc. It was not until 1891, that North Yamhill finally got around to recording a plot map with the county and declaring itself a town and started collecting taxes. This town without a proprietor had about ten businesses in 1871 and twenty-eight businesses listed in a McKenney's Pacific Coast Directory in 1883. The spirit of the old west had prevailed. The very first businesses were on West Third Street in the late 1850s.

Yamhill County Historical Society Collection
The above building was the Yamhill Education Company School, built in 1869. After it was purchased by Yamhill District 16 in 1880 the bell tower was added. The building was replaced in 1894 by the building shown on page 63.

Chapter 5

Is There a Ghost on Alex Butte?

As mentioned before, this book is a story of the area around Yamhill. Most of the stories were related to me by my relatives from several generations, most of them were long time residents of the area.

The history of any community would be the relating of facts that shaped the physical development of that community. The economic development of any town is influenced by the geographic features of the land surrounding it and the actions of the people who have come in contact with that area. Yamhill had all the usual fires, murders, and unusual "happenings" that occur in all communities. Recently, a young man was tried and convicted of murdering his own grandmother. We have colorful characters like in the early part of the century the person who was a hermaphrodite with equally functioning sex organs. As a very young man, I heard stories of how he would satisfy the needs of loggers who came out of the woods on weekends and kept their wives company during the middle of the week. Over the years there have been many more colorful people who resided in and around Yamhill.

One and a half miles south of Yamhill on Highway 47 there is a small hill about 500 feet high called Alex Butte. It is not named after my great-grandfather, Alexander Fryer, who once owned the site, but after Alexander Carson, a brother of Kit Carson. I first heard this story during the 1930s at Fryer family reunions at the home of William Fryer that was located on the slopes of this interesting geological site. This is now the home of the Chaffees. At these reunions all of my uncles and aunts advised that Alex Carson was a fur trapper. Around 1840 he became separated from the rest of his party as they were traveling down the North Yamhill River. Indians supposedly drove him up the butte and as a last resort, he climbed up a big oak tree. He hid along one of the tree's larger branches. He lay there quietly but as would happen,

Gordon Zimmerman Photo

Alex Butte (880 Feet) is in the center of the picture. Notice the ridge of the Coast Range about twenty miles west and seen on each side of the butte. Fryer Road is on the left.

he sneezed. The Indians pulled him from the tree and scalped him. Soon other members of his party arrived and were advised what happened before he died. The legend goes that he was buried under a stone cairn, a very big pile of rocks.

Over the years many people have searched all over this butte during all seasons of the year for a cairn of rocks. This grave has never been found. I personally question this legend because of just one point of the story. Where are the rocks scattered all around the area that could have been used by Alex party of trappers to construct a stone cairn? Today the lower slopes of this hill are farmed. There are many large oak trees along the upper part of this butte, but inspection shows there are no rocks or even gravel around the entire area. There is nothing but loose soil on this butte.

In 1996, the Yamhill County Historical Society published an article by John White about a legend of a ghost on Alex Butte. Mr. White had done extensive research on many historical aspects of many areas around Yamhill County. This research is respected by all. Mr. White's research has shown that Alexander Carson was a cousin of Kit Carson, not a brother. Dates would indicate that Alex was most likely an older cousin of Kit Carson. Alex was an indentured gunsmith who accompanied the 1811 William Price Hunt Brigade of the American Fur Trading (Astor) Company expedition. Their trading posts were established in Astoria and along the Willamette River, one being near present day Champoeg State Park. Alex Carson was one of four Astor Company traders who established this post during 1811. After this company was purchased by the Hudson Bay Company, somehow Alex escaped the slavery imposed on fellow Astor Company employees by the benevolent dictatorship of Hudson Bay Company. He was able to operate on a freelance basis and was able to trade with Hudson Bay. Up until the early 1830s his name also appears in this company's records as occasionally accompanying their forces from Fort Vancouver into distant regions such as the Grand Tetons and Spanish California. From several accounts it appears he was a shrewd trader and a very hard worker.

Sometime around 1834, Carson decided to build a "Wintering Hut" on the butte that now carries his name. From here, he could travel much of what is now Western Oregon, trading with Indians from spring to fall and return to his cabin to spend winter in reasonable comfort. A major advantage was that it was on a major Hudson Bay Company trail from Fort Vancouver that went over Cornelius Pass and Bald Peak and through Cove Orchard Gap. This became the first all land wagon road from the Portland area to Yamhill.

Carson eventually hired a Tualatin Indian named Boney to help him. As was the custom Boney's wife and young son would accompany the two men on their extended journeys. It is believed that while on the trail Alex and Boney would sometimes split up for days, affording Alex the opportunity to go back to camp for an affair with Boney's wife.

In the winter of 1835-6 Carson fell seriously ill and was unable to leave for his spring trading journey. He then decided Boney and his son should depart on schedule while Carson stayed behind for a while to recoup under the care of Mrs. Boney.

Whatever suspicions Boney may have had concerning the joint interests of his wife and employer were confirmed after a chance meeting on the trail with Click-kowan, a Tillamook Indian, who had passed Carson's cabin a few days earlier. He reported Alex appeared to be reasonably healthy, but neither he nor Boney's wife seemed to be in any particular hurry to catch up with Boney. Now enraged, Boney, his son, and Click-kowan returned to the cabin where they captured and brutally tortured Carson to death. Details of this deed came from a much later account given by the Tillamook Indian. A party of Hudson Bay Company traders passing the cabin in May, 1836, found Carson's cabin burned along with Carson's mutilated remains. The Boney family was never seen again in that area.

Long after settlement of the North Yamhill River Valley began during the 1840s there are accounts that people continued to tell of nights when long, eerie and chilling wails could be heard moving through the trees on Alex Butte. Also, some spoke of sinister, dark shadows resembling the shape of a man appearing to dance in and out of a thick mist that would form behind the ridge. Was it the dismembered ghost of Alex Carson roaming the butte seeking revenge upon his vicious killers or was it an evening breeze through the oak grove in fog?

Early residents of Yamhill and all living members of my family who have lived on or near the butte have been given the facts from Mr. White's article and none of us has heard of or seen a ghost on this butte. We will leave it up to you to decide if Alexander Carson was scalped because he had an affair with his employee's wife or because he sneezed. Take your pick. Is there a ghost on Alex Butte? Where are enough rocks for a stone cairn? You be the judge.

Chapter 6

A Railroad Comes to Yamhill

During the last few years, research has been done on the development of railroads in Yamhill and Washington Counties. It has been a fascinating subject. We find our railroads were built as an important part of the complete Pacific Northwest system, not just little local use only lines. A bewildering profusion of railroad names were involved. It took over twenty years, from April 15, 1868, to build a railroad from Portland to Hillsboro, then south through Gaston and Yamhill to St. Joseph and Whiteson. From there the ring of steel around Chehalem Mountain was finally closed via Newberg and back to Portland on July 23, 1888.

During this time, railroad construction had been involved with two gauges and many individual companies. Some of these companies were legitimate working companies and some were just a front for 'paper' companies. Many fortunes were lost. It was par for the course to lie, swindle, and cheat, in other words, just the common everyday way of doing business in those days. Remember that there was no Securities and Exchange Commission, Interstate Commerce Commission, or hardly any other state or federal governing bodies controlling those 'birds'. It was every man for himself and the one who could scheme, lie, and 'pull a fast one', were most often the ones who would win out. Many of the people involved were what we would now call 'suede shoe' promoters and definitely not people of sound business judgment investing their own money for the good of the communities involved.

To present a clear detail of what transpired, I will present the development of the railroads in chronological order from 1846, to present day. I will bring in other companies not directly related with the construction of the ring of steel around Chehalem Mountain, because they will be a part of this story at a later date.

So, let's go — turn the pages of time back to 1846, and the first mention of a railroad in Western Oregon that I could find. That is the year George Wilkes got a bill introduced in Congress to build a railroad from the Missouri River to the Columbia River and to establish military posts along this route to be selected by the military. He was too far ahead of the times and his bill got nowhere.

In 1850, H. M. Knighton, the original owner of St. Helens township proposed to strengthen the claim of his city, as the seaport head of navigation on the Columbia River, by building a railroad from St. Helens to Lafayette. At that time Lafayette was the largest and predominant town in the Willamette Valley, much larger than the city of Portland. (River traffic then was the only year round transportation.) The proposed railroad was to go over Cornelius Pass.

This proposal quickly stirred up William W. Chapmans who proposed to build a railroad from Portland to Lafayette, also during 1850. He got a little further than Knighton in his proposal. Chapmans is given the distinction of organizing the first railroad company in the Willamette Valley. He called it the Portland and Valley and he actually got stock subscribed. Both of these railroads were premature and went nowhere. There were many, many more railroad names dreamed up before this railroad odyssey was over.

After Chapmans' Portland and Valley RR got nowhere in 1850, the Oregon Legislature granted charters to no less than four railroad companies in 1854. One was down the west side, one down the east side; one was to some coal deposits in Polk County at a place called Cincinnati, now called Dallas. The last line was to build from Oregon City Falls to Portland. None of these lines were ever built. They were still way too early even though the legislature helped organize the companies. The only railroad trackage to be built in Oregon during the next sixteen years was a very short portage railroad around the falls at Oregon City. It was called the Willamette Falls Railroad. Motive power — horses! However, there was a lot of talking, surveying, investing, and dreaming.

Jumping ahead to January 1863 our neighbors to the South in California were very busy. This is when Central Pacific started construction of a railroad from Sacramento to the East, eventually to connect up with the Union Pacific. They hadn't even reached the foothills east of Sacramento until the town of Marysville, then the headwaters of navigation on the Sacramento River, began agitating for a branch from the new main line near Newcastle. When it became apparent this branch would undoubtedly be built, talk started about closing the 400-mile gap between the Sacramento River and the Willamette River in Oregon. Everyone was getting railroad fever during this period of growth after the Civil War.

Enter now Simon G. Elliott of Marysville, the villain of this story as far as Washington and Yamhill Counties are concerned. He actually got a lot accomplished toward building a railroad, but turned out to be a liar and a cheat. It has become clear that he didn't know anything about building railroads. He was a 'suede shoe' promoter. In April 1863, he went to Oregon to interest the people of the state in a preliminary survey. He had no success in raising money until a member of his party, a Colonel Charles Barry met Joseph Gaston in Jacksonville. Gaston became most interested and immediately raised a large sum of money. Elliott and Barry returned to Marysville and spent the summer surveying north with a party of thirteen men.

However, before Elliott returned north he pulled the first of his 'fast ones'. He helped organize a railroad company, the California and Oregon Railroad Company, to build a railroad from Marysville to the Oregon border, taking with him not only all money subscriptions from California, but also money raised by Gaston for the Oregon survey. By November 1863, the survey party had reached Jacksonville. That fall and winter, Gaston was still interested enough in the project that he went out and raised enough additional funds to continue the survey on North to Portland the next year. That fall they incorporated another company, the California and Columbia River Railroad. By late 1864 the survey reached Eugene. There, Elliott and Gaston had a falling out. Elliott said the survey was going through Salem. Gaston and Barry said they were going through Polk, Yamhill, and Washington Counties to Portland. At this point all survey work ceased for four more years. The project had simply run out of interest and money when surveys began to show the immense cost of the project.

As far as Oregon's rail history is concerned, the next important date to remember, in fact the most important date of all is July 25, 1866, when Congress enacted a bill granting lands to aid in construction of a railroad and telegraph line from Portland, Oregon to the Central Pacific Railroad in California. Elliott's California and Oregon Railroad Company was to build that portion of the line located in California. The Oregon portion was to be built by "Such company organized under the laws of Oregon as the legislature of that state shall designate." It granted twenty alternate sections of land per mile, ten on each side of the road, in a checkerboard pattern.

The race was on! Gaston immediately dug out his old Barry survey and incorporated the Oregon Central Railroad with the aid of his former ally, Barry. The articles of incorporation were filed with the Oregon Secretary of State, a Mr. S. C. May. On October 6, 1866, May endorsed the original incorporation papers. Remember that this was in the days before Xerox machines, and any copies had to be written by hand. Gaston took the papers back from May and went to the legislature, then in session on October 10th. He got the Oregon Central appointed as the railroad to comply under the terms of the Congressional Act.

It was clear sailing for Gaston. Well, not quite. Enter Elliott, always in search of a buck. He returned to Portland after an absence of several years and right after he had been squeezed out of the California and Oregon by "The Big Four". He and some Salem interests formed another company also called the Oregon Central Railroad and filed incorporation papers with Secretary of State May on November 17, 1866, listing no investors and with no available money. Gaston to strengthen his own incorporation documents, went back to Secretary May with signatures of many very influential incorporators, May endorsed the papers as of November 21, 1866, and kept them. May then removed or blacked out the old date of October 6. Gaston did not realize it at the time, but he had just been had. May had pulled a fast one. After all his home was in Salem, not on the Westside. "I am not making this up, you know!"(Anna Russell's famous quote describing Wagner's Ring Cycle.)

After the stock market crash of October 1929, Southern Pacific Railroad put a number of key personnel in all divisions to writing a history of SP and all its predecessor companies. They had them do this instead of laying them off since there was no work. It was SP's form of welfare at the time. The extremely detailed history that was written was only published a little each month during the 1930s in the SP bulletin, Sunset. Most of the information just given is from those papers.

If you think it has been complicated up to now, well it certainly has not been in comparison to what went on for the next four years. Because of May's juggling of the records, the Eastsiders went back to the legislators and said they should be appointed the recipient of the land grant because Gaston was not incorporated until November 21st and there was no Oregon Central in existence when they gave Gaston the rights on November 10th. Real nice!

Now suits and counter-suits really started to fly. I mercifully will omit fifteen pages of fine print from the history just mentioned earlier. During all of this, Gaston, as usual was out raising some money. He got the City of Portland and Washington, Yamhill, and Polk Counties to respond. He got Yamhill County to give $75,000.00, an enormous sum, at the time.

Elliott went to San Francisco to sell stock. When he came back, he claimed he had a commitment from Alfred J. Cook for five million worth of stock to be purchased for two million in cash. So the big day arrived. The Westsiders held a ground breaking April 15, 1868, at 4th and Marquam Hill Road. Thousands were in attendance. Parades were held and speeches were made. Not to be outdone, the next day the Eastsiders had a ground breaking at what is now SP's Brooklyn yard. There were more parades, more speeches — "Portland's now really on the move", sound familiar? But it was one big poker game. Neither of the groups had any cash money in hand, nor did the line go anywhere.

Gaston soon proved that Albert J. Cook did not even exist when Elliott tried to show he had a second three million-dollar commitment from Cook. By then, both companies were in default of the terms of the 1866 land grant. Congress and the State of Oregon rejected both companies' claims.

Earlier Elliott had sold a 4/10 share of his railroad to a B. Goldsmith in Portland; then sold the same 4/10 share to a N. P. Perrine in San Francisco. In the summer of 1868 Elliott demanded an additional sum from Perrine equal to 4/10's of summer expenses. Perrine had already had enough of Elliott and sold his 4/10's share to Ben Holladay who was selling his Pony Express and stage lines.

Mr. Holladay also owned steamship lines and was becoming interested in Oregon railroading as the completion of the overland railroad in 1869 would put his stage line out of business as a carrier between railheads. As the East, West Overland Railroad became operational, there was a tremendous rush to establish stage and freight lines running north and south from this new method of transport. An example of these rail lines is the line between Cheyenne to Denver and on south and Corrine, Utah, (just west of Ogden), which quickly became one of the largest towns on the railroad. It was this railhead that was used for the mines in Montana and Idaho. Holladay made immense profits disposing of his horses, wagons and equipment at just this time.

Holladay arrived in Portland September 12, 1868. He demanded a controlling interest in the company. He promptly bought out some minor stockholders and demanded to meet Albert J. Cook. Elliott had met his match, for when Cook could not be produced, Holladay paid Elliott $21,000.00 he supposedly had furnished Cook, and Holladay was now in control. He fired Elliott as a director, but he gave him a job for $500.00 per month as chief engineer and sent him out to grade his railroad.

It did not take Holladay long to realize something was wrong. He called on a road engineer friend who had helped to build the Central Pacific, and requested that he inspect Elliott's work. He reported to Holladay that the bridges were all incorrectly built and would collapse under the weight of the first train. The fills and roadbed would wash out when it rained, (they actually did that first winter), and in places he did not even stay upon the purchased right of way. Holladay acted very fast. That was the end of Elliott on the Oregon Railroad scene. This man who had caused Gaston so many problems and probably changed the demographics of the western part of the Willamette Valley to this day was finally exposed. He was all hot air and was fired.

During the spring of 1869, Holladay got Congress to re-establish the land grant. He tried to get it all for himself. However, Congress said that whichever Oregon Central could build the first twenty miles of track would get the grant.

Holladay had most of his road graded by time rail arrived, and on October 28, 1869, they started laying rails. Another gala ground breaking was held in Portland at First and Clay Street. New Era, about twenty miles out, was reached on Christmas Day, 1869. Holladay had won! Gaston had his Oregon Central graded to Hillsboro, but he had no ties, no rails, no engines or equipment and no more money.

But Gaston was not through yet. He must have been a very dynamic man. Remember this was 1869, and it was railroad mania time. The Civil War was over. The gold spike had just been driven May 10, at Promontory Utah. The transcontinental railroad had been completed. With the coming of a railroad, towns would not be so isolated. Trains were a true wonder to behold. Every town in the country was striving to get a train. When they got one, massive celebrations were held with 90 to 300% of a town's recorded population showing up.

With all this railroad interest, hope springs eternal for Joseph Gaston. A man named B. J. Pengra had been promoting a railroad from Eugene to Winnemucca, Nevada through Alturas. Another group was promoting a railroad from Astoria to Salem. After he lost his land grant bid to Holladay in very early 1870, Gaston got these two groups together. All agreed to build a line from Astoria to Forest Grove, use Gaston's Oregon Central from Forest Grove to Portland, continue south through Forest Grove through Yamhill to the McMinnville area and then to Corvallis and Eugene. From Eugene the line would proceed southeast through Oakridge, Lakeview, Alturas, and on to the Central Pacific at Winnemucca. The Oregon delegation thought they would have no problem getting a land grant through Congress for this project. The Central Pacific said they would build it if the land grant could be secured. However, Holladay got wind of it and he sent a delegation to Washington, and the land grant was defeated from the McMinnville area south to Winnemucca. Gaston had to be content for a land grant from Portland to Forest Grove and from Astoria to the McMinnville area.

At this point Gaston gave up the fight. You could say he saw the handwriting on the wall. On July 2, 1870, he sold the west side Oregon Central to Holladay. Holladay had just reorganized the shaky east side Oregon Central into a legal firm, Oregon & California Railroad. He was then able to sell eleven million dollars worth of bonds to German investors. Salem was reached just in time for the fair and a massive celebration.

A newspaper article was printed about the train's arrival at the Oregon State Fair in Salem. Exhibitors complained that every time a train whistle would blow, everybody abandoned the other fair attractions and went running over to the nearby tracks to see this new wonder of wonders. After all, everyone in attendance had walked or rode a horse to the fairgrounds. Here was this machine that could travel twelve times faster than a walking pace of three miles per hour; it is no wonder that they were in awe of the machine.

The year 1871 found lots of activity on Holladay's roads. The road was built south of Salem to Eugene. In addition, the road finally got out of Portland on the west side, this time with rails, on to Hillsboro. The year 1872 was even better. The railroad arrived in Gaston in September, near North Yamhill in October and finally reached St. Joseph just east of the junction of North and South Yamhill River on November 3, 1872 under the direction of Joseph Gaston. Gaston had

Gordon Zimmerman Photo

Photo taken September 2002 at South Yamhill River Bridge south of McMinnville, Oregon. This High Iron Tour was the first train with paying passengers stopping in McMinnville since 1929, sleeping there in Pullmans.

Yamhill County Historical Society Collection

The Mesner hack waiting to return to the Southern Pacific Depot in front of the Hotel Royal, Yamhill.

been hired by Holladay and was the supervisor of construction from Portland to St. Joseph. All work stopped at this point for eight years.

While Gaston was building through North Yamhill, he used a ploy that has been used by railroad builders many times before and since. Even though North Yamhill was the only town around, when a subsidy of $10,000 was not raised, the railroad was routed three fourths of a mile east of town. From the time the railroad opened, horse drawn hacks or taxis delivered passengers to downtown Yamhill.

A mile south of the North Yamhill Station, Joseph Gaston met a sharp negotiator in Alexander Fryer. When it came time for Gaston to purchase over eight acres across the Fryer farm, Gaston had to pay $150 for this right-of-way. Records indicate only about $50 was paid for a like amount of land to other farmers north of the Fryer Farm. This is the Century Farm where I live.

Two towns were established, both construction sites for building the railroad, St. Joseph, and Gaston. Although other people may have suggested these names, there is little doubt who they honored.

It had come to light that the eleven million dollars worth of bonds had been sold for 50 cents on the dollar. There were four million more for the westside line that had sold for even less. Interest was now coming due. Revenue was far under what was anticipated. Holladay at first stabilized the railroads with the profits from his steamship lines. The German bondholders soon heard of Holladay's financial problems. Henry Villard, a former German war correspondent covering the Civil War was sent to see what was happening. The investors tried to work with Holladay for four years. Finally on April 19, 1876, the bondholders foreclosed and Holladay faded from the picture.

Holladay had proved that he was quite a man, but his business practices were not financially sound. He spent money with a grand flourish, without logical reasoning. His properties did not earn even a small part of the interest involved in acquiring them. However, he contributed very much to the development of the Willamette Valley. His colorful life-style is well documented in early Oregon history. Besides his railroad interests, he bought out the long established steamboat line on the Willamette. Holladay then floated an $800,000 loan and consolidated his ocean and river lines into the Oregon Steamship Company. Additionally, he started a daily newspaper and a real estate company. He launched a terminal warehouse and transfer business as a private venture; sufficient

Southern Pacific Railroad Photo
Yamhill Station built in 1872, transfer point for freight and passengers to Tillamook.

Yamhill County Historical Society Collection
Old Station at Carlton taken just before the Red Electric trains started in 1911. Southern Pacific advertising called this route "The Road of a Thousand Wonders."

earnings being procured by contracts with his railroad and steamship companies. Certainly his program was an ambitious one. By the fall of 1872, Holladay had enthroned himself as the absolute ruler of all lines of transportation on land, by river or sea in Western Oregon, except the Columbia River, where he had to compete with the Oregon Steam Navigation Company. For eight years he had ruled supreme in Oregon. But his power had rested on a shaky foundation. Holladay's business practices and extravagant life-style left him penniless when he died.

It was Villard's turn next and he reigned supreme for eleven years as Oregon's transportation czar. He surpassed by many times the number of miles of new railroad that had been constructed by Holladay. Oregon was about to witness a frenzy of new railroad construction.

From 1873 to 1876 during Holladay's slow collapse, Villard had made several trips to the Willamette Valley and Portland areas. It is reported that he was enthralled with the area. It was so much like the area around Frankfurt, the home of most of the bondholders, only without people. On his first trip back to Germany, he immediately set up an immigration office in New York, Boston, and in Germany to encourage more people to move out here.

In the eleven years from 1873 until 1884, Villard accomplished more than any man before or since in the advancement of Oregon's transportation system. He promptly organized the Oregon Railway & Navigation Co. He bought out Captain John Ainsworth's Oregon Steam Navigation Company that consisted of two portage railroads at what is now Cascade Locks and The Dalles. He promptly started construction of a railroad from Portland east following the south bank of the Columbia River.

One of Villard's most fearsome competitors was the Northern Pacific who could use the north bank of the Columbia. As the railroad was getting closer, he made his move. Villard by then had the unprecedented confidence of investors; he asked for eight million dollars in a blind pool, not divulging its purpose. It was immediately over subscribed — he received eleven million. With the money, he gained controlling interest of the Northern Pacific. Try that one on your local banker today.

Meanwhile back in Yamhill and Polk Counties, the natives were getting restless. Villard had done nothing about building south from St. Joseph. They were growing large crops of grain and were becoming tired of hauling their cargoes through the incredible Willamette Valley mud holes to the Yamhill River at Dayton or the railhead at St. Joseph, near McMinnville.

Beside the railroad, another easing of the problems of shipping agricultural crops from Yamhill County occurred just two months after the opening of the railroad to St. Joseph, giving the railroad a form of competition. On January 1, 1873, locks around the 40-foot falls on the Willamette River at Oregon City were opened. All during the time Gaston was building a railroad on the west side, The People's Transportation Company was blasting four locks on the west side of the river. Now it was possible to have a single boat service from Lafayette to downtown Portland. This brought about tremendous savings in shipping costs from Yamhill County. The Corps of Engineers eventually purchased the locks in 1915 from Portland Railway Light & Power. Since the 1850s there had been a short portage railroad around the falls, motive power — horses. Primitive, but it did the job.

The opening of the locks at Oregon City, may have helped in transporting crops, but the mud holes were still everywhere, closing all movement for around four months a year or more. The area of western Yamhill County was very fertile and it was felt that one million bushels of wheat could be grown on this land. In 1875, local farmers contacted Joseph Gaston. Soon a narrow gauge railroad was started from the Dayton Wharf to Sheridan. Amity, the only town along the route, should have observed what Gaston did to North Yamhill. When the city fathers did not give him a $5,000.00 subsidy, he routed the rail line two miles north and west of their town. The line opened on October 24, 1878.

It was not until January 1879, that the Henry Villard interests opened a 49.7-mile line on south of St. Joseph to Corvallis.

By 1881 Villard was riding high. He now had a controlling interest in Northern Pacific and was building from Portland up the Columbia River. He made a deal with Union Pacific's Oregon Short Line and was to meet them on their westward trek across Idaho. They agreed to meet at Huntington, Oregon near the eastern Oregon Border.

About this time Villard sold his interests in his steamship company with a sizable profit. The German bondholders were also forthcoming with additional investments. In order to get more traffic on the railroad, he had to get to Ashland and join the Big 4's

California and Oregon coming up from Marysville. Work was resumed on the Oregon and California south of Roseburg.

By 1883, the O & C had finally reached Grants Pass. Villard's Northern Pacific drove its golden spike August 22, 1883, in western Montana. On September 8 a massive celebration attended by thousands with four special trains was held at Gold Creek, Montana. However, there had been huge cost overruns on both the NP and the O & C projects. Drive the Cow Creek Canyon Road from Riddle to Glendale and Wolf Creek and you can see this amazing piece of railroad. All built by hand.

A whispering campaign was started stating Villard was in trouble. His stock value dropped to just a fraction of their former value. By juggling his shipping interests, he managed to persevere. O & C reached Ashland on May 4, 1884.

Some historians say the UP and CP gave Villard a little shove into bankruptcy now that he had almost reached his goals in eastern and southern Oregon. He had a top heavy debt structure. He had almost arrived at the agreed meeting points only to be told his connections were still three years away. UP & CP were strong enough to wait. Within three months Villard would crash.

Villard continued to struggle on during the summer, grading on up the Siskiyou Mountains. He had drilled 500 feet of the Buck Rock Summit Tunnel when construction under his management stopped in August 1884. His financial pyramid collapsed. His connection with the Oregon & California was at an end. Today, he remains one of the primary forces that took a railroad from Portland to both the eastern and southern parts of the state. However, he was not finished in the financial world. In 1889, he organized Edison General Electric Company and acquired control of Edison Lamp Company. He died in 1900.

Chapter 7

The Most Awful Ride in the World

During 1872, the stage was set for North Yamhill to become a transportation center for the northwest part of the Willamette Valley. Joseph Gaston's Oregon Central Railroad had arrived. Just a few months before the arrival of the railroad, James and Thaddeus Quick had incorporated the Trask River Wagon Toll Road Company. The stated business of the corporation was the construction and maintenance of a wagon road or pack trail from North Yamhill west to Fairdale, (now the Flying M Ranch), to the 1660 foot summit of the Coast Mountains. Here, they would travel down the Trask River to Tillamook. This was the most direct route to the Oregon Coast and a small harbor deep enough to accommodate shallow draft, ocean going sailing schooners. It is believed that this 45-mile road was open for wagons, not just pack animals, by 1876, as a local newspaper listed tolls for horses and stage passengers.

Thus, the town of North Yamhill became the gateway to Tillamook County. Mail was carried on packhorses to Tillamook, right after the road opened. Tillamook became a sub post office of North Yamhill. It was now possible to take a boat from Corvallis and Albany to Champoeg, then on up the Yamhill River to Lafayette. Here there was transportation available for the short six miles to North Yamhill. The train from Portland made direct connections with the stagecoaches and freight wagons to the downtown area of North Yamhill. Here, several livery stables rented horses and any kind of horse drawn vehicle that one might desire.

According to the *Yamhill Reporter* of August 17, 1882, at least one public conveyance was running at that time on a regular schedule over the Trask Toll Road: "The hack for Tillamook leaves North Yamhill on Tuesday's and Friday's at 2:00 P.M., stopping overnight at Summit House."

Yamhill County Historical Society Collection
Mesner's stage used on the Tillamook route. The stage is parked in front of Hope Perry's home on West Third Street in Yamhill.

The hotel business was always good, and other services thrived. North Yamhill was a busy place, containing about thirty businesses. All this, and it was still a town without a proprietor. As mentioned earlier, the town did not incorporate until 1891.

Yamhill now had a road to the west that fit the dictionary definition of a road: "Road: a public or private way, usually maintained by a private railroad or government or toll authority for the passage of persons, animals, or vehicles during all seasons of the year. Such ways are called railroads, highways, streets, avenues, place, alleys, etc."

Yamhill now had a railroad to the north and south. It had roads north, south, east, and west. The citizens were now not so isolated.

Experienced racecar drivers today have nothing to worry about compared to the Trask Mountain stagecoach drivers. It would be difficult for most people to realize that one person could handle four to six ribbons of leather to the bits in the mouths of his horses, control the often hard to manipulate brakes, keep a gun close at hand, sound the horn for stops and blind curves, soothe the nervous passengers, and keep the stage on the embankment and out of the river. Racecar driving seems so easy!

Trask Mountain Stage – 1906.

Just before this book went to press, a gentleman related a fascinating story to me of the many freight wagons that operated between the Southern Pacific Yamhill Depot and Tillamook. He advised that all information that he had seen about the toll road only talked about the passenger stages with no mention of the extensive freight movements over this road. He advised that his grandfather was one of many freight wagon drivers over this route.

It is known that the Southern Pacific Railroad made L.C.L. (less than carload) shipments into all of the valley's towns from the lines opening in 1872 until the late 1930s when the station agents were removed. At least five wagons a day hauled all kinds of freight from Yamhill Depot, including general Merchandise from stores in Portland to businesses in Tillamook. It was by far the fastest way to move merchandise into that area. He advised that there were a number of freight wagons on this road every day in all kinds of weather. This would account for the continuing operation of four hotels evenly spaced across this mountain, not feasible if there were only one passenger stage a day using this road.

The Carlton & Coast Railroad opened in 1910 to Tillamook Gate, about three miles northwest of the Flying M Ranch. Here, it crossed the Trask Toll Road and was designated a common carrier only to this point. Carloads of freight were shipped to this stop from 1910 until the railroad was opened to Tillamook, November 1, 1911. During this time the teamsters stayed overnight at 16 Mile House or Travelers Rest Hotel at Fairdale, instead of Yamhill.

It was not until the railroad opened to Tillamook that it received it's own postoffice. From the time the first pack trails had opened over Trask Mountain, Tillamook had been a sub-post office of Yamhill.

Chapter 8

Yamhill Faces a New Century

By the turn of the century, North Yamhill had every reason to be proud. A brand new Methodist Church had just been constructed during 1898, built mainly with funds furnished by my grandfather. The town was now a legally incorporated city, and it had become almost the largest town west of Portland. The town had about forty businesses and boasted of several establishments and services usually found only in a town of a much larger size. A large new public

Celia Dromgoole Collection

This picture was taken July 4, 1898 at Maple Street between First and Second Streets. Beginning from right, Farmer's & Merchant's Bank built in 1880s now Bella Café. Next Horce Robert's Hardware Building torn down in the 1960s. Next building is still standing and the next was removed in the 1920s. Note: Every building has a different width.

Pat Heflin Collection
Hauswirth & Bedwell Store, Main and Maple Streets, site of the present day T & E store, Chamberlin Hotel and John Lemarr Saloon, right.

Pat Heflin Collection
Johnston & Hutchcroft Store, S. Maple and First Streets, now site of Zippy's. The top floor burned off about 1937 and was rebuilt as a one-storey building.

Yamhill School built in 1894. This picture was taken in 1906, when the school held grades one thru ten. Note the large belfry that held one of the three bells in Yamhill from Verdun, France.

school had opened in 1894. It was stated that Mary Smith, who would later become Mary Pickford, lived here in 1900 with her mother, a teacher at this school. However, this was not the first school to be built on this site. In fact, it was believed to be the third school at this location.

The very first school to be opened in Yamhill County was one and one half miles northwest of Lafayette. The Hembree and Millican families built it in 1844. Classes were suspended when their children had grown up by 1850.

The donation land claim law came into effect by 1850. News of this did not reach the West until well into 1851. It stated that to hold and to keep new and even older claims, a family had actually to live on the land. Many had been living in towns. This is why that by 1852 new schools were being built all over Yamhill County wherever there were a few settlers close enough that children could walk to class.

Ruth Stoller's book, *Schools of Old Yamhill,* states that according to original survey maps there were three schools in the north Yamhill area by 1852. One would have been what became District #1, Pioneer School on the North Yamhill-Lafayette Road at the east end of the now abandoned Merchant Road at Yamhill Road. (This road should never have been abandoned since to this day it would be the shortest route from Forest Grove to Yamhill and on to Salem.) The second school on this site still stands. It was built in 1916 and is now a residence.

Another North Yamhill School (the second to be built) was west of the village one mile on what is now Pike Road. The third school built in 1853 is believed to have been built on the 1894 site and is said to have been a log cabin as were other schools in the county.

Ruth Stoller states in her book that North Yamhill has one of the most interesting histories in the county because when public funds were lacking, private corporations would erect school buildings. The first school building other than a log cabin in the town of North Yamhill was the project of the North Yamhill Education Company. It put up a two story Academy building in 1869 and operated it for several years. The Education Company sold this building, including three acres, to District 16 in 1880 for $1, 300.00. Public School District 16 had been operating since 1853 west of town near Pike Road. It is believed that the North Yamhill Education Company was a school for Non-believers. By the 1860s most towns around the county had schools sponsored by various churches such as the Quakers, Congregationalists, and Baptists. By the 1880s Frank Hauswirth built a Non-believers' school just south of where the Methodist Church is today.

About 1900, Non-believers built another school in what is now the Knight of Pythias (K-P) Hall. I remember that the main floor of this building still had blackboards from the school until the 1930s. I also recall that my grandmother spoke with great disdain about "those" people who did not go to church and had to have their own school. They were heathens!

The first separate high school building was constructed in 1936. The author was in the first class to occupy this building for all four years, graduating in 1941. The 1894 building was not replaced until 1950. In 2002 the high school was remodeled to bring the 1936 building up to current code. This included six new classrooms added on the upper level of the original gymnasium. The city of Yamhill can be very proud of its present day schools.

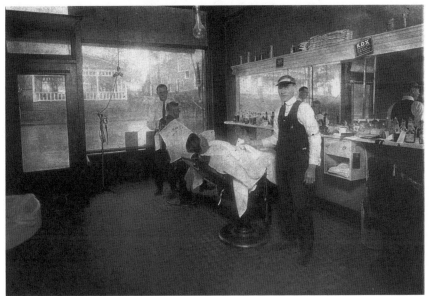

Ben Reimers, right foreground, owned Yamhill's Barber Shop from 1917 until 1935. The building here seen through the left windows at 160 S. Maple was Yamhill's Bandstand. Note the corner of Hotel Royal at right. The mirrored backbar is still in the town's current barber shop.

Yamhill never had a plaza in the middle of town. The closest we had to a plaza was a bandstand on the corner of our banker Norris Perkins' property next door to the Hotel Royal. This was across the street from the town's major retail stores.

This became a town of many firsts. In 1902, D. P. Trullinger installed a small dam and dynamo west of town on the Yamhill River, making Yamhill the first small town in the state with electric lights. In the same year, Yamhill had the first rural mail delivery in Oregon. In 1907, Yamhill was the first small town with rural telephones, the first town with concrete paved streets, with cement from Holland, and had the first high-wheeled delivery truck in the state of Oregon. Much earlier, in 1847, this town had the first flour mill driven by waterpower using stones from France that had been purchased by John McLoughlin. They came around the Horn in 1847. Also, the first herd of purebred Holstein cattle were brought to Yamhill and Oregon by the soon to be first postmaster of Yamhill, Benjamin E. Stewart, via the Isthmus of Panama to San Francisco and then overland in 1847. Most amazing, occurring also in 1847, Yamhill had the first lawful registered distillery and U.S. bonded warehouse for aging "spirits" established in the state.

Miss Dolly's Girls Collection

This home was built in 1884 for D. P. Trullinger. It was located on a knoll just west of Yamhill at the junction of Moores Valley Road and Oak Ridge Road.

Gordon Zimmerman Photo

This set of milling stones came around the horn from France and for years were at the Whitman Mission. After the massacre they were set up on Oak Ridge Road west of Yamhill about 1847 for a gris mill beside the river. They were in use for many years until they wore out. When the mill was torn down and the road widened, ther stones were later moved to the Yamhill County Historical Society in Lafayette.

At a meeting, April 13, 1908, the city council of North Yamhill changed its name to Yamhill. Over forty years ago, Mildred Withcombe, a former long time postal employee advised the author that this name change was done at the request of the postal service. Mail was always being misdirected between North Yamhill and North Yakima. Hence, both names were changed. Handwriting was even worse at that time than it is now.

Times were prosperous; coal had been discovered east of town. All though this was a major find, it was never developed. It was so volatile that a drill hitting the coal set the coal on fire. The mine burned for several years. A drill bit with a diamond end the size of a walnut is still buried in the mine.

Yamhill County Historical Society Collection

Miners at the coal mine which operated for a short time near Woodland Loop and Laughlin Road east of Yamhill.

Yamhill County Historical Society Collection
The Hotel Royal, built in 1902, was removed in 1937. The ornate back bar
was moved across the street into the building that is now Zippy's.

In the spring of 1902, fire destroyed the major hotel in North
Yamhill; a small structure built in the 1880s. Even before the fire,
prominent towns people believed the lack of a good hotel reflected
badly on the entire community. They had raised the sum of $2,200
with which to entice a first class hotel. Shortly after the fire, E. F.
Schneider, a local jeweler, inventor and prune dryer owner took up
the challenge.

The North Yamhill Record on August 2, 1902 stated: "The upper story of the Royal Hotel, that contained ten rooms on this floor, is
entirely finished and is magnificent. There is no better-equipped hos-
telry in Oregon; save perhaps Portland. The Tillamook Stage ticket
office is on the first floor and is now operating daily." It was at this
time "Yamhill against the World" became the town slogan.

For the next nine years Yamhill prospered. It was a constant
battle to maintain and gravel the road to Tillamook. Throughout these
years the Trask River Road became extremely important to the settle-
ments in Tillamook County. The stage, which had only been robbed
once, had a number of owners and achieved the nickname of "The
Most Awful Ride in the World." However, the grim reality of geography set in when the alternate route that was available was considered.

Yamhill County Historical Society Collection

John William's livery stable at First and Maple. The boardwalk is now the sidewalk at the City Hall.

Yamhill County Historical Society Collection

Yamhill State Bank building opening day in 1912. The automobile was Frank Worthman's of McMinnville. He drove his car to many opening day ceremonies all over Yamhill County at that time.

That was to take a sailing ship from Portland to Astoria, then cross the treacherous Columbia River Bar, and go south in a small sailing ship that had to be small enough to cross the even more treacherous and shallow bar at the mouth of Tillamook Bay. Every year the Tillamook Bar would be closed six to eight weeks at a time. It could take almost a week to make the trip, and that was in good weather. Over the years there was much loss of life at the Tillamook Bar. Sudden storms would come up while the small ships were at sea. Small wonder that "The Most Awful Ride in the World" looked most attractive. Our pioneer ancestors were indeed a hardy lot, who only traveled when necessary. No matter how much effort was involved, they found a way to get to their destination.

And travel they did. From 1873 there was rail passenger service through Yamhill. There were some resorts throughout Western Oregon. For over 100 years, the favorite resort for our area was the Oregon Coast. However, getting there was truly a problem. The first route to the coast was the Trask Mountain road. However, this was more for business travelers and not for families on vacation. It had been possible to travel by train to Corvallis since 1880. During 1887 a railroad was completed from Corvallis to Yaquina at the headwaters of Yaquina Bay. The line never went any further west because of the narrow ledge at Newport waterfront. A steamboat took passengers the last two miles to the city center. Regular and excursion trains were operating to Newport, connecting with trains from the north at Corvallis.

The next way to the coast was the opening of the railroad from Portland to Seaside in 1898. The line from Astoria to Seaside was built in 1890 by Uncle Billy Reid and was the first part of a proposed line to run up the Nehalem River, through a shoulder of Saddle Mountain and connecting with Harriman's railroad at Hillsboro. Reid's line to Hillsboro was never built. Instead, Hill's interests purchased Reid's Astoria to Seaside line on foreclosure.

The line to Astoria and Seaside was opened in 1898. From Portland to Seaside was 118 miles. It was an instant success for family vacations. The railroad ran several trains a day including "Daddy" trains that left Portland at 2:30 P.M. on Saturday. Most men had to work until noon on Saturday before they could join their families for the weekend.

November 1, 1911 was the last day for the stage coach over Trask Mountain and the first day of operation of the train from Hillsboro to Tillamook. Rockaway Beach on this line became an

The Masonic Lodge building at Third and S. Maple Streets. It housed the third oldest Masonic Lodge in Oregon, having been established in 1851 in Lafayette and moved to this site in 1902. The building was wrecked by the winds of the 1962 Columbus Day Storm.

instant success as a destination resort. Southern Pacific soon operated several trains a day including the Saturday afternoon "Daddy" trains with many extra sections every Sunday afternoons in season. In those days people wanted to do something different on their days off, as they continue to do now.

During 1907, my grandmother's brother, Willie Fryer purchased an oak grove of trees along the south side of Yamhill that is now the Yamhill City Park. He established the Holiness Association tent revival and also called protracted meetings. There was a camp ground surrounding the central circus tent. Revival meetings were conducted for several periods during the summer. People would bring their own tents and other camping equipment in the baggage car of the train and Mesner's hack would take the family to the campgrounds. People came to these Yamhill meetings from a very large area by train and by automobile. There were few state parks in the mountains in those days that were accessible by auto or train. There were revival tent and camp meetings at several places around the valley. They were very inexpensive ways to spend a family vacation away from the city and were accessible by train or primitive automobile.

By the 1930s, there were just a few of these tent revival meetings in this grove. The city purchased the grounds as a city park in 1926. The last meeting I remember was during August 1933. The preacher allowed a fund raising rally to use his tent on a Saturday afternoon for my Uncle Peter Zimmerman's campaign for governor.

The Holiness Association camp meetings fell out of favor with the advent of more automobiles. Families could find other places available for a vacation by driving the family car. Many cars were now more powerful and could drive into the mountains, unlike the Model T's which had to back up steep hills.

In writing this book, a large travel poster dated 1923 could not be located that advertised a new way to go from our valley to the beach. Across the top in large letters it said, "**NEW SERVICE**" "Take Southern Pacific's Red Electric train to Whiteson Junction. Here, you will board the **NEW**, all steel through train to Sheridan, Willamina and direct to Grand Ronde without changing trains. Here, you will board a **NEW** White Company open top bus (as used in our National Parks) for the short scenic drive over the Coast Range Mountains to the **NEW** resort town of Pacific City on the sparkling Pacific Ocean. This **NEW** service is provided by the **NEW** Willamina & Grand Ronde Railroad."

Every word NEW was enlarged and in darker print than the other letters. In the center of the poster, was a picture of a White Bus with everybody waving and with Haystack rock and other beach scenes across the bottom. It has been at least thirty years since I have seen this poster.

By today's standards, a ride in an open top bus on a very rough, dusty gravel road for about twenty-nine miles would not be appreciated by today's standards. In traveling Highway 18 for years to the family's beach house at Lincoln City, I had always wondered why there was such an imposing two story station at Grand Ronde. Upon seeing this poster, I could understand the still standing station's history and know once again that our ancestors were indeed a hardy lot.

Chapter 9

A Railroad Starts Building
Towards Tillamook

By 1905 E. H. Harriman, who owned the Union Pacific and Southern Pacific Railroads, woke up and realized that others had started to build a railroad from his Southern Pacific owned line at Hillsboro, with an announced destination of Seaside. He dispatched Elmer Elm Lytle to purchase the stockholder's interest in this line. Lytle was an established Harriman employee having built a rail line from the Columbia River to Shaniko, Oregon for the Harriman controlled Oregon Railway and Navigation Company in 1897. He had also worked as a station agent for this Harriman Road.

On October 13, 1905, Lytle incorporated the Pacific Railway and Navigation Company. Harriman was up to his old tricks as he was not listed as a backer. Lytle immediately changed the route of the railroad from Hillsboro to Seaside, to Hillsboro to Wheeler. There had been rumors that James J. Hill of the Great Northern Railroad, who now controlled the railroad from Portland to Astoria, and Seaside was now interested in building a railroad from Seaside to Newport or even further south to better compete with Harriman's steamships out of Newport to San Francisco. Lytle purchased all oceanfront property a railroad could use from Wheeler to Tillamook, particularly all rocky headlands to block Hills's efforts of building down the Oregon Coast.

Lytle was ordered to proceed at all costs. It did not seem to matter to them that they were building a railroad over a pass that was in excess of 1800 feet high. (To this day this pass is over 200 feet higher than any other major crossing, has significantly more maintenance, trestles and tunnels than other routes that were available). This route is about thirty miles longer for freight that was heading south to the SP than a railroad down the Trask River would have been.

The threat from Hill was real and had to be stopped. Harriman accomplished his goal. Hill never completed the railroad from Seaside to Newport.

Harriman spent five million dollars building from Hillsboro to Tillamook, an unbelievable amount for those early days. On traveling the route today, it is very easy to see why construction costs were so great. One must remember that this was just four years before the Hill and Harriman forces were building railroads up the opposite sides of the Deschutes River by day and battling each other by night. It was a colorful time in Oregon's history.

The railroad was transferred from the dummy company, Pacific Railway and Navigation Company, to the Southern Pacific Line in 1915. This was a common working arrangement used by Southern Pacific all over the Western United States when building new roads. The line was opened November 1, 1911. The final run of the stagecoach over the Trask Mountain from Yamhill was the same day.

Harriman may have stopped Hill from building south from Seaside, but he did not stop Hill from competing. By 1915, Hill had built a dock at Flavel located half way between Warrington and Hammond at Tansey Point on the Fort Stevens Branch, near the mouth of the Columbia River. Two large very fast ocean liners, costing three million dollars each, were constructed and given the names of Great

Yamhill County Historical Society Collection

The last stage over Trask Mountain, November 1, 1911, leaving Tillamook Post Office for Yamhill.

Northern and Northern Pacific. These ships traveled from Flavel to San Francisco in just twenty-six hours. A first class round trip ticket from Chicago to San Francisco was just $90. One would take a regular NP or GN train to Portland, board a special train to ship side at Flavel and be in San Francisco overnight in just a short time longer than it took to ride the Southern Pacific train to San Francisco over the slow Siskiyou Mountain passes. During 1916 my grandfather returned from San Francisco on this ship. In later years he often talked about this journey, his only trip on the ocean.

Most people do not realize that even to this day the economy of Tillamook is affected by the long ago battle between Hill and Harriman and their competition for travel routes from Seaside and Tillamook to Portland. The battle was to continue and the ties between Tillamook and Yamhill Counties took a new direction.

In 1906, William A. Howe of Carlton started a sawmill three miles south of Yamhill in Carlton. He dammed the North Yamhill River west of Yamhill, and with the aid of a number of flashboard dams, he literally flushed the logs down the river to a lake in Carlton. By 1909, he realized that this scheme was not practicable. The logs kept ending up in farmers' fields where it was expensive to retrieve them and kept washing out D. P. Trullinger's hydroelectric dam west of Yamhill. As an alternative, he started to build the Carlton & Coast Railroad. His aim was to build a railroad into the timber country to

Pat Heflin Collection

D. P. Trullinger's dam for his electric power generation plant and water powered gris mill constructed near this site in 1857. Covered bridge over North Yamhill River in background.

Tillamook County Historical Society Collection
Trask House. It burned in the 1933 Tillamook Burn.

Tillamook County Historical Society Collection
Summit House on Trask Mountain Road.

Tillamook County Historical Society Collection

Fairdale mineral springs.

Toll House at Fairdale - Left to Right John A. (Shorty) Sampson, Mildred Sampson, John Kay Sampson

Tillamook County Historical Society Collection

Traveller's Rest at Fairdale.

Yamhill County Historical Society Collection

The Carlton & Coast railroad depot in Carlton about 1910. These people are waiting for the Sunday picnic train into the woods.

Pat Heflin Collection

Vulcan saddle-tank engine during the short time the Carlton & Coast was called Flora Logging Company.

bring out logs for his mill and to build on to the Oregon Coast as the name inferred. In a short time, his road was east of the summit, about thirty-five miles from Tillamook, some down the easy and open Trask River grade. He knew that Lytle was bogged down getting over the mountains. An attempt was made to get a small amount of additional financing in these prosperous times. Even with the help of Charles Ladd; the son of William Ladd of Portland's Ladd and Tilden Bank (the largest bank in Portland, which had interest in the Carlton Mill), the money could not be raised. It is known that the hand of Harriman was everywhere. At one station before Tillamook Gate, Fairchilds, he gave up building to Tillamook and built his railroad as a logging line with steep four and five percent grades and a switchback. This line about thirty miles shorter to the Willamette Valley was never built. It is obvious that Harriman was not about to let a short upstart railroad gain access to the Tillamook market first. Once again the Trask River Canyon, the only canyon that ran straight east from Tillamook to-wards Portland would continue to remain silent. Until 1939, the author remembers seeing the log trains headed to Carlton from Tillamook Summit area traveling just a quarter mile west of Alex Butte.

Photo by Clarence Mitchell

Pete Focillio, left, is the foreman for this Italian track maintenance crew on the Carlton & Coast, circa 1915-1920.

It was not until twenty-one years later that new hope was raised to use the Trask for a direct route east. *The Oregonian*, on January 8, 1928, devoted its entire front page to a map showing all possible routes between Portland and the coast. By January 20, 1931, *The Oregonian* printed a state highway commission report showing the shortest route to be the Trask — Tualatin River route through Yamhill or Gaston. However, it recommended a route from Gales Creek to

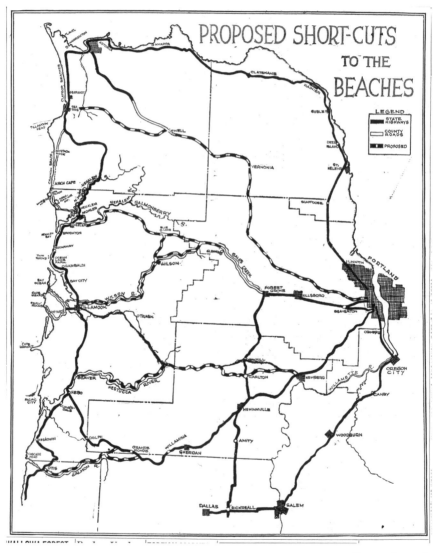

Oregon Journal

Suggested new road from Portland to Coast – 1928.

Wheeler, only one route to be built to serve Seaside, Astoria and Tillamook. By August 16, 1931, in the *Oregon Journal*, a state recommendation was made that two roads be built. First one would go from Seaside up Wolf Creek to near Banks. The only way it would be possible to finance this direct route from Seaside was for a second road from Tillamook to follow the Wilson River to near Banks, then share a joint road to Portland. Many citizens in Tillamook were furious. The route was about ten miles longer than a direct Trask-Tualatin River road to Portland via Farmington Road and the North slope of Bald Peak. It made traveling south down the Willamette Valley to such points as the state capital in Salem about thirty miles longer per trip. Over the years, Tillamook has paid dearly for this compromise that so benefited Seaside. At the time, many of the farmers in Tillamook area felt that this was just too high a price to pay so "a bunch of city slickers from Portland could go out and lay on the beach at Seaside." They had farms to run and the shortest road to get to hay and grain in the Willamette Valley is what they wanted. The Wilson River was so much longer and crossed the mountains almost 1000 feet higher than a road up the Nestucca River. Remember trucks during this time were small and under powered by today's standards.

I remember attending a grange meeting with my father in the early 1930s in Tillamook. It was a meeting with farmers and members of the state highway department at which time the proposed Wilson River Highway was being explained. To this day, I have never seen a group of people expressing such anger and disgust at those conducting a public meeting. The locals pointed out that a Wilson River route was so much longer to get to the Willamette Valley and the state capital at Salem. They also knew that the road would wash out because this river carried so much more water than any other coastal streams. It has washed out — many times!

The eventual choice of the Wilson River Route has been disastrous for Tillamook. Over the years this road has been closed for weeks and months at a time from washouts and land slides. The last closure in 1996 cost about $50,000,000 to re-open. It was closed for over six months. Now there is talk of improving the only 900-foot elevation Nestucca River Road that runs directly west from Yamhill.

So to this day, only an easy to maintain narrow graveled Forest Service road travels the Trask. It was by-passed twice in this century. The first time by a railroad, then by a major highway that gave others

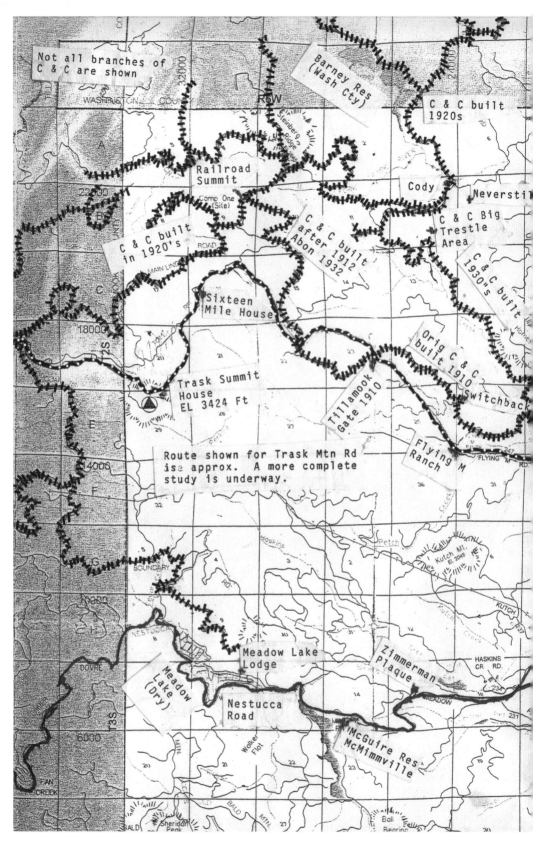

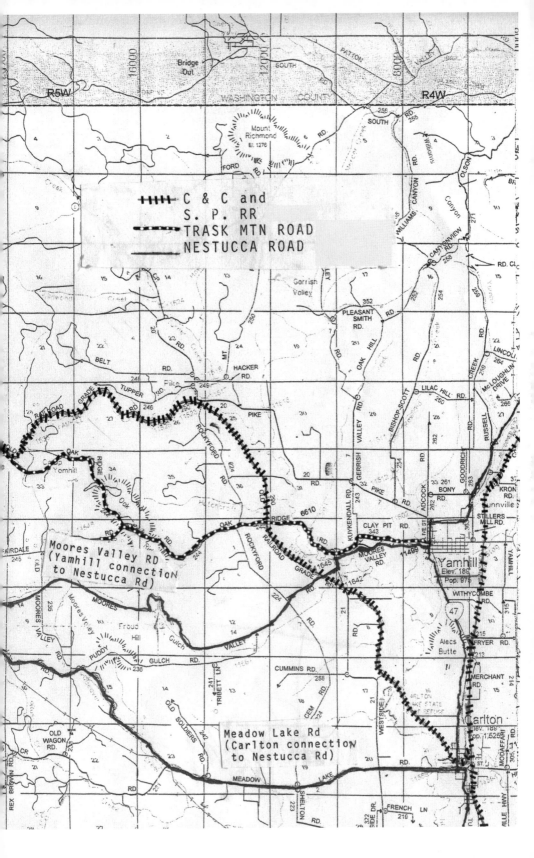

what they wanted. In both cases, people and aspirations from outside the area took control of access to this important Oregon Coastal community. Yamhill was also deprived of being on a major east, west traffic corridor. Tillamook is poorer and the Trask River Canyon continues to sleep as a major traffic corridor.

Chapter 10

Marketing Hogs By Moonlight

In the summer of 1907, my father, George Zimmerman, felt very proud of himself. He was then seventeen years old and his father, Christian Zimmerman let him take a team of horses and a wagon loaded with fat hogs to Portland. For the last several summers he had been accompanying his father to Spaeth's Butcher Shop at SW First and Main Street in downtown Portland. Here they always got top dollar for the hogs, because the shop was owned by his cousin, Emma. George did this about once or twice a year for about ten years. The way he got to Portland was most interesting. He would load the hogs in a wagon that had a liberal amount of straw on the floor. During the late afternoon he would travel to friends of the family, the Guenthers, who lived at the foot of the grade of the road over Bald Peak, now Albertson Road. Here, the hogs were off loaded, fed, watered and bedded down before dark. The next morning at 4:00 A.M., he reloaded the hogs. He went over Bald Peak, crossing the Tualatin River near the present Highway 10 crossing of this river. Here, was a ferry that would hold horses and a wagon. The ferry could be pulled across the river by a rope, hand over hand, or by a winch. The cash for the toll was left in a container nailed to a post.

From the ferry, he went on to Beaverton and down Canyon Road to downtown Portland. Arriving at Spaeth's, he sold the hogs and immediately started back to the Guenther's, arriving by midnight. The next morning he was home by 10:00 A.M.

The reason he went to all this trouble was very simple. In the summer months the roads were always passable. If the hogs were shipped by rail car they would go to the Portland Stockyards and be sold to wholesalers at a lesser price. Also, most importantly, it might take two or more days to get the car to the stockyards. During this time the temperature might go up and the hogs could arrive as cripples. If this happened the difference in price was significant.

My father always advised that it was much easier to time the trips to Portland on nights when the moon was full and bright. He had a hard time getting the horses to travel up the east slope of Bald Peak when it was very dark and the horses were tired.

As a young man, I remember driving hogs for short distances. It is my feeling that no other animal or human can let out such an expressive sigh of relief and look up at you with such contentment as can a fat hog that has been traveling on foot and then lays down. I have always believed that a fat hog thought of the phrase: "Oh, my poor aching feet." Remember, their feet are not much larger than the last joint of a human thumb to support 200 pounds.

During the mid 1930s my father was still making deliveries to Spaeth's Butcher Shop. In these days before wide spread refrigeration, my father would get up early to kill and dress out one to three vealer calves on a Saturday morning. Most of them had been my pets for a short time. He then took me to Portland where he dropped off the calves, let me off for my orthodontist appointment and picked up a load of feed and supplies for the feed store. Woe be to me if I was not ready to be picked up at the Yamhill Street side of the Portland Library at the appointed hour.

Chapter 11

Electric Trains Come to Yamhill

During 1998, a number of city and county governments conducted a study to see if it would be feasible to start a limited commuter rail service from Portland to McMinnville, Oregon. This is not a new concept. Eighty-five years ago, there were up to five electric trains a day between McMinnville, Yamhill, and Portland. They traveled up to seventy miles per hour, arriving in downtown in less time than it can be accomplished today during commute hours. Is this progress?

In 1912, James J. Hill of Great Northern and Edward Harriman who at that time owned Union Pacific and Southern Pacific were at each other's throats again. There had been some form of steam passenger service in this area ever since the rail line was opened to Yamhill in 1872.

In an effort to counter growing competition for regional passenger service, Harriman of Southern Pacific began to electrify its west side main lines through the Willamette Valley. James J. Hill had just opened a brand new, electrified railroad down the east side of the valley though Salem, Albany and Eugene during 1912. It was an instant success. He called the line the Oregon Electric. He earlier had opened a branch to Forest Grove in late 1908.

Harriman could see the success of the O. E. He started a project that would eventually cost him $1,600,000 to electrify all of his west side lines. The west side division ran from Portland to Beaverton, Forest Grove, Yamhill and to St. Joseph. Here he electrified his ring of steel around Chehalem Mountain back to Portland by way of Newberg, Tualatin and Lake Oswego. This portion was called the east side division. From St. Joseph the electrification continued south on a single line to McMinnville and Corvallis.

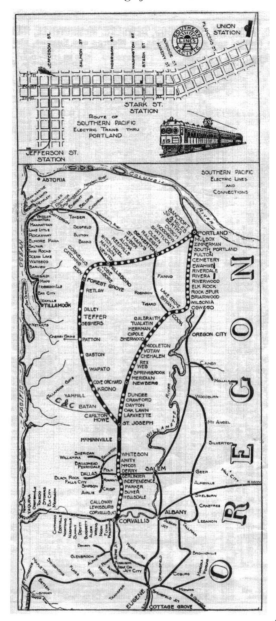

Al Haij Collection

This timetable of May 5, 1925, shows all electrified lines of the Portland to Corvallis. Krono is the site of the Zimmerman Century Farm and Batan is the site of the Fryer Century Farm. The line from Beaverton to Portland was torn up and became Barbur Boulevard in the 1930s. Note the long way around for freight to move south out of Tillamook. In 1930 the electric cars were sent to Los Angeles where they served another thirty years. On Sundays, one could travel from Portland to McMinnville via both routes for $1.50.

The service was called the "Red Electrics." Barn red paint was applied to these units operating on the west side of the Willamette River. This contrasted to the O. E.'s dull green on the cars operating on the east side of the river.

The grand opening for this seventy mile per hour electric operation was January 18, 1914. Some special excursion fares around the loop to McMinnville were advertised as low as $1.50 on Sundays. It was a great day for Yamhill County, resembling the Fourth of July celebration in every town. People could now travel with incredible speed with no fear of mud. Everybody felt it was a service that would operate for all time.

For a number of years these trains prospered. The decline started in 1921. There had already been a road over Rex Hill to Portland. However, in 1921, Highway 47 opened between McMinnville and Forest Grove. The entire twenty-five miles was a 24-foot wide concrete surface road and had only about twelve curves that would cause one to slow down to about forty miles per hour. At the time, many people thought it was a waste of money. It was too wide, too straight, could have gone over little hills and had a gravel surface, this being an entirely adequate road for the day. It is almost all still in use today.

Yamhill County Historical Society Collection
The Southern Pacific Red Electrics on left, went into service through Yamhill in 1914. Steam train to Willamina on right at Whiteson Junction.

Up to this time it had been easier to go from Yamhill to Portland by way of Albertson Road over Bald Peak. The mud still had been too thick north of Gaston through the Tualatin River wetlands to Forest Grove.

After 1921, there was a steady decline of revenue for the electric trains. By that time improved trucks and tractors to haul gravel had been invented. The bottomless mud holes were not so treacherous. Trucks could also haul express. As the new state highway department built more roads throughout the 1920s, the steady decline continued for the Red Electrics, and also for the O. E.

By 1927, Southern Pacific could see the "handwriting on the wall." They established the SP Motor Transport Division and started the silver and gray (not red) painted Oregon Motor Stages. At the time everybody thought that this was an upstart company giving SP some competition. The ploy worked. The last electric train through Yamhill was July 28, 1929. However, a steam powered passenger and express train was started and operated through Yamhill until 1933. During 1914, when they opened, everybody just knew these seventy mph, beautiful, red trains would last for all time. They lasted for only fifteen years.

Chapter 12

Where is the Steam Engine?

Around the first of November 1919, my father was elected to the Yamhill County Board of Commissioners. One of his first projects was to persuade the state to locate the soon to be under construction Highway 47 over 100 feet further west of the Cove Orchard sink hole that had been contemplated by the very young engineers of the just created State Highway Department. They had not done their homework in consulting with the railroad about their problems at this location. Over the years this point had been a nightmare for the SP. This moving the road further west worked. The original concrete surface was covered with a layer of asphalt for the first time during the 1960s. There was no sign of concrete settling at that time.

This sinkhole is located at the exact point in Cove Orchard Gap where the Tualatin River watershed flows north and a creek flows south into the Yamhill River. It is about one quarter mile north of the Cove Orchard store where the highway veers about 150 feet west of the railroad, then immediately turns back to continue running beside the right of way. The core of the sinkhole is about 10 by 25 feet running at a 45-degree angle from the now abandoned railroad right of way. Until about the 1960s no grass would grow on the core. Now grass is growing over the entire area and a single tree grows at the east edge of the core area.

Many times my father enjoyed telling of his first encounter with this natural phenomenon. In the spring of 1894, when the days were still long, a neighbor schoolmate of my father came and got him before school to run over to the sinkhole. Here, an engine had derailed and the front end was in the sinkhole. These two nine-year old boys then ran to school where they got a licking for being late.

As soon as school was over, Willie Little and my father ran back to the sinkhole. Help had arrived. Two large steam powered wrecking cranes had removed the wood filled tender during the day and had set it aside. The two cranes were now trying to remove the engine. It was obvious even to two nine-year old boys that the harder the cranes pulled on the engine, the deeper it was sinking. The cranes pulled on the engine until it was almost dark. A signal was given to abandon the project. Soon the two cranes were steaming away; one pulling the re-railed tender.

It was in the fall of the same year that the west side branch of SP was converted from wood to lignite, a very low grade of coal. It probably came from southeast of the Seattle area or Coos Bay. Both had a very low grade of coal. This event was well remembered by my family as their home was only about 100 feet west of the railroad at Krono Station, one mile north of Yamhill. It was built facing the only method of transportation when it was erected in 1883. My mother advised that all the trains had a huge plume of smoke as they went by the house, caused by burning poor fuel. Many times she mentioned how very glad she was when the line was electrified and when the remaining steam engines were converted to oil in 1913.

My grandfather, Christian Zimmerman, purchased his farm about one mile south of the sinkhole, from the estate of the original homesteader, J. J. Burton. A story passed down from the Burton children to my grandfather states that Joseph Gaston was advised by the Indians not to build across the sinkhole. Both Indians and early settlers had lost horses and cattle in this sinkhole in this only gap through the Chehalem Mountains. He should have listened. Many times over the years the railroad has dumped hundreds of carloads of large rocks and remains of concrete buildings on each side of the railroad, up to about five feet on each side.

From 1919, until the 1960s my father rented the field immediately east of the sinkhole. I remember operating a combine over this dry field in the 1940s. Since the 1980s, the railroad has done no filling. Now all land east of the railroad has sunk so much that the entire area is a wetland.

Where is the steam engine? Probably down a few hundred feet and shifted to the east. It would be impossible to find it even with the most modern metal detectors because of the huge amount of rebar in the concrete from buildings torn down and dumped on the site for about 100 years.

Chapter 13

From Horses to Model T's

My father George Zimmerman graduated from Oregon State University in 1910. He then purchased the family farm from his father. A few years later, to augment his income, he started to purchase livestock from surrounding farmers. When he had acquired the proper amount, the livestock would be loaded into a railroad car for shipment to Portland stockyards. He often explained how he would load a car for the 6:00 A.M. freight train. He would then jump on his horse to ride to his home one mile north; do the chores, eat breakfast, take a

C. Roy Fryer Photo

Zimmernanville — By 1930 members of the Zimmerman family owned about sixty percent of all the land surface area shown in this picture. The gap in the middle is Cove Orchard Gap. C. Zimmerman's new home is to the right of the tree line below his prune orchard shown at bottom. The prune dryer (upper left) is to the left of center. Note the end of paving. The car is passing horses. Note the poles to the right of the barn for SP Electric trains at Krono. Bony Road & Hwy. 47 is at the small building in the center of the picture, one mile north of Yamhill. This is the south edge of George Zimmerman's farm.

bath, and catch the morning Red Electric Train to Portland in front of his house at Krono station. He would arrive at the stockyards before noon. His car of livestock would generally be there shortly after, around 1:00 P.M.

As an outgrowth of his thriving cattle brokerage business, in 1916, he and his brother, Edward, opened Zimmerman Brothers Grain Company and built a 25,000-bushel grain elevator on the railroad at Yamhill. A big problem with the stock brokerage business was the area farmers' inability to have access to a reliable source of grain for feed and sundry items to operate their farms. This business operated in Yamhill for the next sixty-five years.

He continued to buy stock until 1920. During this time, about 1917, he purchased sixty-one head of 200-pound fat hogs from Pleasant A. Smith, five miles northwest of Yamhill. Right after he purchased them, there was a heavy rain. The roads were now too muddy to haul the pigs by truck. It was still cool, so it was decided to drive them the five miles to Yamhill's railroad yards. By the time the pigs were ready to load the next morning, they would not move and only squealed when prodded. My father had to put a sling under them and carry them on board. When they got to Portland, the pigs had to be carried to the scales and sold as cripples at a great financial loss.

Yamhill County Historical Society Collection
The building at the extreme left was used by Zimmerman Brother's retail feed store from 1925 until 1940. Both buildings were on the site of Sterling Savings Bank today.

For three years he had been begging the county to work on the roads in northern Yamhill County. During 1919, he decided to run for County Commissioner. He ran on ticket of improving these roads. He won by a margin of twenty-eight to one. Try that nowadays.

During the previous three years, he had decided just which roads should be changed. Up to this time all roads went up and over all available hills to find the driest land, as explained earlier. In 1920, the entire philosophy of building roads changed. He often heard, "Get those overweight, huge tired Model T's off the road, we can hardly get through with our buggies because our roads are being torn up by all that power." From car owners he heard, "Get our roads off the tops of every hill in sight, and around every section 90-degree corner to a road level and straight." The Model T's could not climb up the 22-degree hills encountered on many county roads.

Thus, in the 1920s, more roads were relocated in Yamhill County than any time before or since. This was greatly aided by the Federal Aid Road Act of 1915, which provided matching grants mainly for rural market and postal roads. My father was very proud that the first federally assisted market road in Yamhill County, and one of the first in the nation, was Market Road #1, now Highway 240 from Yamhill to Newberg, through what was once Ewing Young's Chehalem Valley.

Celia Dromgoole Collection

Will Underwood at left near his team of horses. My aunt Ella and her son Clifford are in his new car, about 1919. Old and new transportation.

This was possible because, in anticipation of his election, he had all the paperwork prepared and ready to submit. In all, he got fourteen roads in Yamhill County relocated under this new program, all using this changed philosophy of road building.

Over the years this area needed an immense amount of gravel to make our roads suitable for travel all times of the year. There were no natural gravel deposits near Yamhill. The only usable rock was from a quarry on the Northwest slope of Bald Peak, eight miles away. The author remembers the special gravel wagon driven by the town's mentally handicapped person, Bill Fairbanks. Before the time of "political correctness" we called these individuals feeble minded, idiots or morons, even to their face. It was the common practice during this time period that most of these disadvantaged individuals were castrated as was Bill. He was a very large man being over six feet tall and weighing over 200 pounds. He always wore a sheepskin coat winter and summer. He said it kept the heat in on cold days and kept the heat out on hot days. Everybody knew Bill as the town character. Many times, in downtown Yamhill, kids chased him and called him names such as "idiot or moron" and sometimes they would trip him. He would try to chase them but he was way too slow to catch them. It did not make any difference to anybody. After all, he was just the town idiot.

For years, Bill worked for my father, George Zimmerman, cultivating and harvesting using horses. Many times, while he was in the horse corral fixing a fence, I saw his horses come over to him and rub his back and otherwise muzzle him. They would follow him around wherever they could. It was very common for horses to get a small rock embedded in a foot. If this happened a horse would lift a foot several times to get Bill's attention so he could remove it. Such is the way with many animals. They understand the differences in people and try to comfort them. He was good at odd jobs during the off-season.

To keep him busy, my father would have him take two horses and a special rock wagon to the Bald Peak quarry. Here, crushed rock would be fed down a chute by hand into the wagon. The wagon was about four feet wide and about ten feet long and would carry a load about three or four feet high.

This wagon had an ingenuous unloading system. The bottom was loose 2" x 6" pieces of lumber installed crosswise of the wagon along the entire bottom and rear gate. With extra long lines controlling the horses, Bill would remove one 2" x 6" at a time allowing gravel to spill out the bottom as the horses slowly walked down the road. He would keep a very even pace as he crawled up into this wagon that was quickly losing its floor and continued to remove one board at just the right time. He did this while handling ever shortening horse reins and balancing his over 200-pound body on each side of this gaping hole. To slip would have meant a leg under a wheel. He could haul only one or two loads a day. A load would only cover about twenty feet of road at the most.

He was complemented often for his even spreading of rock. Neighbors often wanted to borrow the wagon and Bill to rock their driveways. Rock was expensive, hard to transport and would often disappear into bottomless mud holes. My father kept two horses until the late 1930s, long after he had acquired tractors. He did this to be able to give Bill work all during the 1930s.

Bill's mother worked upstairs in our old downtown retail feed store on the present site of Yamhill's bank building. One could still see the outlines of the various rooms in this area when it was one of Yamhill's small hotels. All during the 1930s she used a large sewing machine patching burlap sacks, which were the only way to transport feed and grain to the various farms. She and Bill lived nearby and she took care of him since his birth. He could neither read nor write. Any money he might receive he would spend for candy at the ice cream and candy shop next door to the feed store. His paychecks were always given to his mother.

Mrs. Fairbanks died about 1940. Bill had never taken care of himself in regard to food and shelter. He must have been about fifty years old at that time. He was taken to Fairview Home, the state's hospital for the mentally handicapped. Here, he became a severe problem for state workers. Because of his great size and strength, nobody could get him to do what he did not want to accomplish. One day he went out to the barn containing the home's horses. They had not yet had the money to convert all their farming operation to tractors. The authorities soon discovered his love of animals and his ability to work and talk with horses, including some problem horses that soon were no longer a problem under Bill's care. They soon found he could also work with other farm animals and could work with younger men of like mental capacity. He became a farming teacher and friend to some of these patients. We understand he gave the state no further problems. After having what must have been a lonely and unhappy life, his final days were spent talking with horses and surrounded by people at the school.

Even today Yamhill accepts differences and takes responsibility for the less advantaged. There are now two young adult men that are mentally handicapped. Everyone living in Yamhill knows and protects them. They help the families watch out for them.

During the early part of the century to about 1930 there were two other characters of note living in Yamhill. One first arrived in California with a shipment of men from China to work on the Central Pacific Rail line being built from Sacramento to Utah and a connection with the Union Pacific to create the first transcontinental railroad. Many thousands of men arrived from China. The railroad soon preferred these men because they were young, strong, yet small enough to be lowered over a cliff in baskets to drill holes to be used for blasting.

After the rail line was completed, most of these men from China stayed in California with their countrymen. Most were dumped on the streets of San Francisco. By the mid-1870s, conditions for the Chinese in San Francisco were deplorable. It is believed that it

Evelyn Enger Collection

Louie Loy in Yamhill, circa 1918. He lived from 1826 until 1929. *The Oregonian* carried his obituary, December 17, 1929. Note his shoes are made from boards and old horse harnesses.

Pat Heflin Collection
    Louie Loy at his shack on North Yamhill River. He lived to be over 100
years old.

was at this time that Louie Loy left California and traveled to Yamhill.
It is known that he did odd jobs around town and lived along the
banks of the North Yamhill River just west of town where he had
constructed a shack for himself. He always said that he liked this
place because it reminded him of his home in China. His surround-
ings were very primitive. A five-gallon can served as a stove on which
he cooked roots, herbs, and weeds that he made into soups and
teas. He ate cougars and other wild game as delicacies. He made his
shoes from a piece of board and discarded pieces of leather from
horse harnesses. Records indicate that he was born in 1826. When
he died in 1929 he was a well-known regional character. He would
write to the U.S. presidents currently in office and tell them what
was wrong with the country as seen from Yamhill. He would write
out copies in those days before copy machines and send them to
local newspapers. Amazingly, many letters were answered. When
he died, he was such a well-known character that *The Oregonian*

published his obituary on December 17, 1929. One of the people for which he did odd jobs over a period of years was for Ruth Gallagher, Evelyn Enger's grandmother. Every year, he walked to the Pike cemetery after she died and placed flowers on her grave in a hollowed out stone he had made and placed beside her grave stone. Every year, Evelyn still places flowers in this stone on her grandmother's grave.

Quong Hop is the other person from China who lived in Yamhill from the late 1880s until the late 1920s. He was born in the upper Yangtze River area. When he was about twenty years of age, he took up with a band of sampan nomads and eventually worked his way down river to Changchow. He managed to exist by doing odd jobs along the waterfront.

One day he was told of a tramp steamer in port that was signing up a hundred coolies who would like to go to America at $50.00 each. He had the fare and within two weeks they set sail. He found himself in stuffy and stinking quarters below deck with a hundred bad-tempered and many very seasick companions who were constantly cursing and swearing. After about two weeks [sic], the ship traveled up the Columbia River and anchored near Albina rail yards.

The human cargo was kept out of sight for a week while arrangements could be made for dispersal. Then, three or four at a time they were moved to an abandoned grist mill under cover of night. From there, they were assigned to logging camps, farms, and canneries. Because of his small size Quong Hop was one of the last to leave. He was placed in the home of a hop grower south of Newberg. There, he became a trusted member of the household, responsible for cooking, washing, ironing, and all other house chores. It is believed he stayed there for a number of years.

One summer Quong Hop accompanied his boss to a Hop Grower Association meeting in North Yamhill. While waiting for the meeting to end, Quong Hop talked to some town merchants and found there was an acute shortage of washing and ironing facilities in town. Within a month, his boss had helped him to rent a house on Larch Place, behind the present day City Hall. It had a good 60-foot well, deep for the area. Supplies soon arrived from Portland by rail and he fast became a real part of community life. It is reported that he kept beer at the end of a long rope in his deep well. It was said to be the coldest beer in town.

During World War I, business was so good that he moved to the Sander's Hotel Annex next door to Yamhill Bakery. Here he added a sandwich bar, soda fountain, and candy shop. This building was just south of the building that housed Zimmerman's downtown feed store, now all owned by the bank. It is said that he always maintained an extra bed in his living quarters so people in trouble could stay overnight. He would often loan people money to help them through difficult times. There are still people alive today who remember buying a piece of candy from him for one cent.

My sister, Celia Dromgoole, remembers the May Pole and Flag Day celebrations held every year in front of the school building. These two Chinese gentlemen were always there to tell the children that they were from far off China and how lucky they were to live in such a great town such as Yamhill in the United States.

Quong Hop became ill in the late 1920s and as was the custom of many Chinese people in those days, he returned to China to die. As a young man I heard many stories about this kind, very caring, and generous person.

Pat Heflin Collection

Quan Hop (upper row, left) at GAR Reunion.

Over the years, there have been a number of people who have made some very noteworthy accomplishments. These are newsworthy and have reflected well on the name of Yamhill

Besides Mary Pickford there have been other people of note from Yamhill. During 1939 and 1940, a young lady who graduated from Yamhill High School in 1934 became one of the most photographed persons in the United States. Her name was Zoe Dell Lantis, the theme girl for the San Francisco World's Fair. She was born near and attended Cove Orchard Grade School. Her picture was continually in all of the national magazines and newspapers in bathing suits and a pirate's uniform, the theme of the fair. She repeatedly was interviewed on the radio and she always said that she was from Yamhill, a very beautiful and historic town. When asked how she got the job, she said she just mailed some pictures to the fair and they called her. After the fair she continued her modeling career.

Ken Jernstedt also originates from the Yamhill area. He was a member of the Flying Tigers who flew against the Japanese for the Nationalist Army in China prior to the outbreak of World War II and afterwards. He continues to be interviewed about his wartime exploits. Over the years he has been active in flying circles and recently helped to open the Evergreen Air Museum in McMinnville, where his P-38 is on display. This museum houses the Howard Hughes Spruce Goose, just ten miles south of Jernstedt's hometown of Yamhill.

During 1988, a former resident brought the name of Yamhill to the attention of millions of people throughout the United States. That was the year Beverly Cleary, the famous author of about thirty childrens books, published *A Girl From Yamhill*. Copies of her books number in the millions. For years she had been asked to write about her own childhood. This book became one of her most popular writings. Many consider them to be time capsules.

Beverly's grandfather, John Marion Bunn built the first fine house in Yamhill. It is still standing today at the end of West Third Street. It was the second house in town to have a bathtub.

Beverly was born in 1916 and lived there with her folks until she was six years old. Her mother had set up Yamhill's first library upstairs in the Yamhill State Bank building. At that time, the family gave up farming and moved from Yamhill to the Grant Park and Klickitat Street area of east Portland. Most of her books have been set in that area.

San Francisco History Center, Neg#9698

Zoe Dell Lantis from Yamhill was the theme girl used to generate advance puplicity for the 1939 & 1940 Treasure Island International Exposition in San Francisco. She graduated from Yamhill High School in 1934 and was a friend of the author's sister, Celia Dromgoole. Here, she and Oregon Governor, Charles H. Martin are about to lead a 5000 car caravan from Oregon to the grand opening of the Golden Gate Bridge in May 1937. This caravan had come south on Highway 101, officially opening the last five major Conde McCullough bridges on the Oregon Coast portion of the road. After the fair was underway, she was replaced as the theme girl by Sally Rand and her fans and nude ranch.

In the listing of noted people from Yamhill to the near present, one person stands out from the rest. That is Nicholas Kristof. His father, Ladis, arrived in Oregon as a Romanian refugee in 1958. He saved his money and graduated from Reed College in Political Science. He later received his Ph.D. from the University of Chicago. He is now retired from Portland State University where his wife, Jane, also a Ph.D. has worked.

Nicholas attended Yamhill-Carlton High School where he was active in FFA and was the editor of the school paper as well as student body president. It soon was expanded to a community paper. During this time, he was also writing for the *News-Register* in McMinnville, Oregon. Nicholas completed his college education at Harvard in three years. He was then appointed a Rhodes Scholar in England. Later, he was hired by the *New York Times*. Kristof and his wife were awarded the Pulitzer Prize for their coverage of the Tian An Men massacre in China in 1989. He is now columnist for the *Times*. His nationally syndicated articles frequently appear in *The Oregonian*. He is a remarkable young man and Yamhill is very proud of this international journalist.

Aside from being fortunate in having two college professors as parents, Nicholas may have another factor that added to his success and positive outlook on life. That is geography. His family purchased the former "Doc" Larsen place near the top of the ridge just west of Cove Orchard Gap. The author's grandfather, Christian Zimmerman, once owned a portion of this ridge, now owned by a Zimmerman cousin, Carolyn Larsen. The author can see this place from his century farm, four miles south. This ridge extends east from the main body of the Coast Range and from this place one can look directly south into the main Willamette Valley along the eastern edge of these mountains. The curvature of the earth limits the distance one can see down the valley. An intelligent person raised in that setting could not help but be stimulated to develop a positive outlook on life. The view is awe-inspiring.

Chapter 14

Prunes Reign Supreme

From about 1900 until after World War II, prunes were a major crop in the Yamhill area. Plums are different from prunes and cannot be dried. Prunes that are properly dried can be kept for long periods without further processing. During 1920s, many people made a lot of money on prunes. Willie Fryer had a large four kiln prune dryer. Willie's younger brother, Roy, had two prune dryers. My grandfather Swingle had eighty acres of prunes on what is now my century farm and a four kiln dryer identical to Willie's. My own father had two prune dryers and ninety acres of prunes.

There were many more prune orchards and dryers in the surrounding area. All of them would deliver their dried prunes to the Yamhill Cooperative Prune Growers packing plant just east of the elevator, on the railroad at Yamhill. Here, the prunes were steamed, washed and had defective prunes removed while on a moving platform. They were then conveyed up to a bin over the packaging unit. While they were still warm, the prunes were dropped into 25-pound wooden boxes that were lined with wax paper, pressed, and the lids nailed on with a six nail automatic nailer. The labels were pasted on and most of the time they rolled right on out to a box car via long section of rollers. Over forty cars a year were shipped from Yamhill. During the 1920s business was very good for their "Mistland" brand of prunes. Profuse yields of wild berries, crab apples, hazelnuts, cherries, and gardens had told Yamhill farmers they had special resources for growing fruit crops. They tried Italian prunes and had a winner. Growing in virgin soils, Italian prune trees would yield three tons per acre. Dehydrated at 175 degrees F, they yield that amount in dried prunes, i.e. one ton (2000 pounds) per acre. At seven cents per pound, $140 per acre in 1915 money, this was a good enterprise. World War I boosted the price to twenty cents per pound.

Changing tastes in the U.S.A., the U.S.S.R. taking over Eastern Europe, and malnutrition of the prune trees killed Yamhill's prune industry. It takes lots of minerals to build the big pits in Italian prunes. In the pre-fertilizer era, Yamhill's prune growers did not realize that they had a problem until after the market was gone.

All during the period from about 1910 to 1945 the picking of prunes was a major event in all of Yamhill County. First, the orchards were leveled and made free of clods of soil. Men with long poles with metal hooks on the end would shake the fruit from each limb to the ground as various sections of the orchard ripened. The season generally started about August 25th. Jobs were created for many people including whole families with many pre-teenage children. During the desperate Depression whole carloads of families would look for picking jobs. Sometimes they were all needed. Some years, we soon had all the pickers we could use and it was heart breaking to turn so many people away. During World War II, I would drive a truck to a labor camp south of Dayton and pick up from ten to twenty-five men from Mexico to pick prunes and haul prunes from the orchard to the dryer. They were very good workers. We could not have gotten through the war years without their help.

Celia Dromgoole Collection

Three kiln prune dryer built about 1914 by George Zimmerman. This building burned in 1940. There were about one hundred of these dryers in the North Willamette Valley. The author almost burned in this building while retrieving a time book at onset of fire.

Some years, if the prunes were late ripening, area schools were delayed up to two weeks. There would have been no use in having them open. They would have been half empty. The children made enough to buy school clothes and other things for school. The going picking rate was ten cents per box. A few families would make eight to ten dollars per day, an enormous sum. Workers in prune dryers made $2.50 per ten-hour day. General farm workers made $1.00 per 10- or 12-hour days. It was a sad day when a law was passed that children could not work in the fields with their parents.

By the late 1930s, the wrinkled funny looking fruit was falling out of favor with American customers. By that time eastern European countries were buying a good percentage of the crop.

After the beginning of World War II, I remember working in the prune packing plant for a number of days. One end of all boxes had been stamped with the size; such as 25-35 or 35-45, etc., which denoted the number of prunes per pound. I applied paste to a label and stuck it on the other end of the box, then stenciled the top with a United States Army number. Why is this a part of our story? Here in Yamhill, Oregon, during a violent rainstorm, I was affixing labels to Yamhill area prunes that read: "Genuine California Sun Dried Prunes from San Jose, California. Grown in the sunny, beautiful Santa Clara Valley." So much for truth in labeling in those days.

Celia Dromgoole Collection
At least twice this amount of four-foot fir wood was needed to fire the prune dryer during a normal season. Dried prunes are in the sacks.

Gordon Zimmerman Photo

One of the last prune dryers to be destroyed by fire was William Fryer's, here seen burning about 1952. It was located on the north slope of Alex Butte across the highway from the author's home.

Gordon Zimmerman Photo

Yamhill Co-op prune packing plant built in 1910. It was sold to Zimmerman Grain about 1951. Still standing today.

The prune business was good until the war ended in 1945. When Russia took over the Eastern European countries that purchased most of our prunes and the Iron Curtain came down, it was almost the end of the prune industry. Within a year, all members of my family had removed almost all of their prune trees. The prune packing plant still stands today beside the abandoned railroad. The words, "Yamhill Cooperative Prune Growers," can still be made out high on the overhead. This building was purchased by our grain company for seed storage and later used for fertilizer storage. It is now owned by an electrical contractor and used as a warehouse.

A companion crop for many prune growers was hops. Hops produce vines that are trained to grow up trellises about fifteen feet above ground. Hops are used in the production of malt that in turn is an important ingredient in the making of beer. Prunes do not like wet feet. Most prune growers that had good bottomland, and a good subterranean source of water, would plant hops next to their prune orchards on the hills.

There were a number of hop yards next to the North Yamhill River. George Sharp had a prune and hop dryer on Russell Creek Road. Bill Newenschwander and Bill Tucker both had prune and

Pat Heflin Collection

Early Yamhill area hop dryer. Note that it is a completely different type of construction than that of prune dryers.

hop dryers on the north end of Laughlin Road. Prune and hop dryers were of a completely different construction. There were at least eight hop dryers around Yamhill.

Hops matured about the same time as prunes. It was not much fun stripping hops off the vines. Pickers applied a protective tape on their fingers. It did little good. It would take years before Johns-Manville invented duct tape that would stick to fingers. It is not much fun picking hops. Besides, about $1.00 a day was all that you could earn and your fingers would be raw for weeks. Today hops are grown in the Willamette Valley, mainly on bottom land along the Willamette River in Marion and Linn Counties; south of Yamhill County.

During 1885, Phillipe Withycombe, originally from England, established east of Yamhill the "Yamhill Tile Works" near what is now east First and Ash Streets, a short distance west of the train station. At this site a large kiln was constructed with accompanying buildings. They manufactured a complete range of clay products consisting of field tile, square building tile, flat paving squares, a 6" square x 13" long, six-hole section cavity tile which were used to build the Yamhill State Bank building, the T & E Store and the store next door. They were also used to create the large heat chambers that contained the wood stoves and piping under each kiln for all the areas prune and hop dryers. All the buildings were built with this distinctive tile that was in turn faced with standard brick. Hundreds of thousands of tiles and bricks were manufactured for use all over Yamhill County and all of Oregon.

Yamhill County Historical Collection
Withycombe Tile Factory, 1885-1933.

The clay came from a pit one half mile west of Yamhill on what is now Clay Pit Road. The author remembers climbing around this large pit in the mid-1930s. The pit has been filled and no trace of it can be seen today.

Clay was always hauled the one mile from the pit to the kiln by horses and wagon. One of my earliest memories is seeing this wagon on Main Street in Yamhill. The wagon was very beat up looking, and was dripping water out of the bottom. The pit had an apparatus to drag the clay from the pit into the wagon.

In the early 1930s, the boiler in the steam plant blew up. Mr. Withycombe was then a very old man and none of his sons were interested in the business. This was the beginning of the Depression, also, Mr. Withycombe died in 1933. The buildings were torn down during the late 1930s and during the war years were used for lumber salvage.

This Yamhill industry that was in business for forty-five years, has, like the prune and hop industries, left a lasting legacy in the north half of Yamhill County and western Washington County.

Mr. Withycomb also operated Yamhill's first processor of milk. Some time before World War I, he opened Yamhill Creamery. It was located at the corner of his property at E. Main and Ash Streets. He operated until the larger Carlton Creamery was opened. Only a small portion of this building's concrete foundation can now be seen.

The coming of the depression greatly impacted all industries in our area.

Chapter 15

The Desperate Depression

By all accounts, the Depression came late to Yamhill, but when it did, about 1935-36, life became very difficult. My father's brother, Peter Zimmerman, was a state senator during the 1930s. In 1933 Joe Dunn, who many thought to be dishonest, won the Republican primary for governor. Many conservative Republicans were so alarmed at his winning the primary that they persuaded Pete Zimmerman to run for governor to take Republican votes away form Joe Dunn to prevent him from winning the election. Charles Martin, the Democrat, would then be elected instead of Joe Dunn. A few weeks before the election it looked like Pete might actually win. He ended up losing by only about 2,000 votes. However, the

Newspaper cartoon published during Mr. Zimmerman's campaign.

    In 1933, the author's Uncle Peter Zimmerman a life long republican was asked to run for governor as an independent. Many felt the republican candidate, Joe Dunn, was a waterfront crook. Peter lost to Charles Martin by only 2000 votes.

original plan was achieved. Joe Dunn was kept from becoming governor who many felt was a waterfront mobster. Martin won primarily by exclusive use of the new media, the radio.

    Since I was about twelve years old, my father would often tell me to get down to the feed store after school. Eddie Enger worked there as the bookkeeper and also waited on customers. My father and Eddie were about the same height and both were agile men. An indicator of the high regard the community had for each of them is the huge attendance of both of their funerals. Eddie eventually worked for Zimmerman Grain Company until 1981, when we sold the business.

One afternoon, about 1938 both Eddie and my father were making deliveries while I watched the store. Just as I arrived, Albert Nelson, the bank president, called to advise that the company's account was overdrawn. Earlier in the day, Charlie Eustice had advised we could get no more groceries on credit. Just as they were leaving, a gentleman came in and paid Dad $2.50 for the rent of the grade school gym — Dad was chairman of the grade school board. Right after they left, my mother called giving me a long list of groceries to bring home.

When Dad and Eddie returned, I was to learn just how bad conditions were. They had not collected any money for deliveries they had just made. No customers had come into the store, so I did not find out that there was just $0.17 in the big cash register. Dad gave Eddie $0.50 from the school rent money for the gym. He gave me $2.00 to go to the grocery store and buy what I could from Mom's list. Mr. Eustice said, "I see he sent the kid down to buy groceries. Was he afraid to face me?"

We went home. Dad stopped at the garden where he pulled some carrots and beets. He came into the house all smiles saying, "I feel like some carrots and beets tonight." Mom never knew how bad it was. We survived.

Many times over the years, when we would be extremely busy and something came up, causing Eddie or myself to work late, we would look at each other and say, "I'll do it." We remembered the day the whole business had just $0.17 in the till.

During 1935, a CCC camp was opened on land owned by the Mitchell's in Fairdale on an area now containing the stables of the Flying M Ranch. It has been said that of all the programs started by the Roosevelt administration, none other had such a lasting effect and "Bang for the Bucks" than this program. The program was started to put large numbers of young men to work during the Depression working in our national parks and forests. It was not until the 1950s that is was generally realized that the work done by these boys in the 1930s would have been absolutely necessary by that time and at a cost many times more than the entire CCC program.

A great number of the young men sent to Fairdale were from the South. Many brought possum with them. Some were pets and others were to be eaten. When the men were shipped out, many going into the army, the animals were turned loose. Many people claim that this was the beginning of our valley's possum problem. They have several large litters every year. Every few months an aggressive possum follows my housecat through a maze through my basement into my garage and then into my back porch. We do what we have to do. The alternative is that I could not keep a cat. I would soon be overrun with field mice in this 84-year old house in the middle of an 80-acre field.

By the end of the 1950s, the possums had a partner in being a pest in our valley. A program was started in growing nutrias for fur. The selling point was that this fur could be clipped and dyed to look like almost any fur. The program soon failed. The county's authorities requested farmers to kill and bury their animals. They were worthless. Many people turned them loose. Now our valley has two quick breeding rodents. It is costing the area thousands of dollars every year to control them.

My grandfather Swingle and his three brothers and his father homesteaded land at the south end of Langell Valley, forty miles southeast of Klamath Falls. Grandfather always advised that the Captain Jack uprising, the last Indian uprising in the United States, started on their land a few months after they arrived in 1872. Within a few years, they had bought out neighboring claims and were ranching approximately 1600 acres.

Right across the road from their ranch house, during the late 1930s a CCC camp was opened. All the boys were from the greater New York City area. My grandparents had a few milk cows, just enough to supply milk for their household and their ranch hands. One day a young man from the new CCC camp wanted to see how milk came out of a cow. Soon, he was bringing over some friends to see this amazing feat. Some evenings my grandfather would show some of the boys how to ride a horse. Later, the camp director came over to thank him for being so kind to the men. He advised that some of the men arrived so underweight and in such a state of advanced starvation that it took some of the men weeks before they were in any condition to do any work.

Chapter 16

Good Times Return

By 1939, and 1940, the winds of war were causing a stirring of the economy of Yamhill. Logging was expanding at Flora's and other logging operations west of Yamhill. Then disaster struck. A fire started in the south end of the Tillamook Burn and quickly spread to virgin timber up Fairchild Creek, near what is now the Flying M Ranch. This destroyed all the huge trestles on the Carlton and Coast Railroad. Some were the highest single bent wood pole trestles in the country. There were several hundred rail cars and about ten steam engines that were now land locked at a logging camp near the headwaters of the Trask River. Some thought they were locked in forever.

It was around this time that a shipyard was opened in Portland. Claude Perkins held the contract for local school buses. He started to haul people from the Yamhill area to the shipyards in Portland, working around the schedule of the school. He was making so much money that he was embarrassed. A lot of his money was buried in waterproof tin cans in his garden. He and his widow were digging them up from his garden for years.

Many people came into the feed store and started to pay on their very old feed bills. A number of people had earlier tried to deed my father their farms for these bills and a small amount of cash. He refused the offers, saying he did not even have enough money for gas to look after their place after they left. It was like everyone was locked in place by this economic prison. Years later, I had many people tell me they would never have survived the Depression if my father had not carried their feed bill for years.

There was some unseen help. Albert Nelson was president of the Yamhill State Bank. At times, the stress of the bank just got too much for him. The Clarence Mitchell's owned and lived in the former Travelers Rest Hotel at Fairdale from the days of the Trask Mountain Stagecoach. In 1936, they built a cabin for Mr. Nelson on the banks of the North Yamhill near the old hotel. He would stay there for a week or so at a time until he was ready to face customers again; asking him for money the bank did not have. My father had everything he owned in his farm and business mortgaged to the bank. Mr. Nelson kept very close watch on Zimmerman Grain accounts receivable. The bank could not foreclose on my father, as property was worth nothing. The county could not even sell property that had delinquent taxes for years.

The Farmers and Merchants Bank of Yamhill was purchased by Sam Laughlin about the turn of the century. He renamed the bank, The Bank of North Yamhill, and built an imposing two-story building to house this institution. He again changed the name of the bank to Yamhill State Bank about the time the new building was ready to open in 1912. Earlier his father Lee had built an imposing house for his family across from the present grade school. It is still standing today. Norris Perkins, the next bank president, built the large house east of T & E and next door to Sam Laughlin. He had just married Sam's daughter. When it was time to pass to the next generation, Albert Nelson, who had married Norris Perkins' daughter, Beryl, became the next president. When Mr. Perkins died during 1935, there was great apprehension as to just what would happen to the bank in those troubled times. Much later, we found that Mr. Perkins had invested an extra $90,000 to keep the bank open when other small town banks had failed in the area.

Mr. Nelson was such a gentleman that one could go against his wishes and he would still work with you. In 1935, the PWA would advance money to Yamhill at three percent interest to build a new high school. Mr. Nelson wanted only a twelve-room school built, twice the number of rooms then in use at the current school building, including using the top floor and basement for additional classrooms. My father, and the rest of the grade and high school board members wanted the 22-room building recommended by the federal and state officials. Many unofficial Board meetings were held in the old feed store. The voters passed the proposal to build the larger school. Mr. Nelson went along with the vote and did not recriminate against those who voted against his wishes. After all, they all owed the bank money!

Mr. Nelson was not the only bank president of the day for whom the Mitchell's provided comfort and quiet. Frank Wortman, president of the First National Bank of McMinnville had serious medical problems in 1937. The Mitchell's also built him a cabin and cared for his medical needs.

One day in the fall of 1939, I was at the store after school. Mrs. Mitchell came into the feed store and gave my father a check for $300. Earlier, during the Depression, she also tried to sell or mortgage all or portions of the ranch to my father. As I stated earlier, real estate was worthless. She had tears in her eyes. She advised that they had received a contract for cutting cedar telephone poles from their land to replace the poles burned in the recent fire that had destroyed miles of the only telephone service to Tillamook. Mrs. Mitchell promised my father she would pay more money every two weeks. She repeated several times, "Every two weeks we will have more money! Every two weeks we will have more money!" As promised she did until she had paid her entire debt. When she paid, I do not remember who was crying for joy and immense relief the most, my father or Mrs. Mitchell. What I do remember is this really marked the beginning of old debts being repaid as money started trickling in from the trusted members of our community.

In 1971, the Mitchell's son, Bryce took the bold step and converted the family hay fields into an airport for small planes. He and his wife, Barbara then built a rustic lodge. This is now the Flying M Ranch, one of the most famous destination resorts in Oregon. The older Nelson cabin is still in use today. It is the one to the right of the footbridge across the North Fork of the Yamhill River, near the main lodge.

By the summer of 1940, conditions were really improving around Yamhill. Many people were still coming in and paying old bills. Some were paying of their own free will, some needed a little nudge.

There soon developed an interesting cooperation between Albert Nelson at the bank, my father, George Zimmerman, and Charley Eustice who owned the general store. The bank had kept very close track of accounts receivable from both stores. The three men held meetings and compared accounts. They even checked if certain people owed money to merchants in Carlton. By 1940, they

Pat Heflin Collection
The Shaw Sawmill just east of the RR Depot grounds at Yamhill. The Prune
Co-op building is on the extreme right. Note wood planking in lieu of expensive
gravel for lumber storage area. This steam powered mill burned sawdust for fuel,
hence heavy smoke at times.

made up a list of those who lived on just a few acres with no possible
hope of having a viable farming operation. Most had not taken full
time jobs though jobs were everywhere. Many had bills well over
five years old. An effective system of alerting was established. The
targeted people soon found themselves in a back corner of the feed,
grocery, or even the local tavern facing someone from the bank and
the two stores. A number of times I was the alerting runner when
people from the list were spotted in town. They were told to take a
job and to advise where they were working within thirty days or they
would be foreclosed!. The shipyards were advertising for men and
women. Logging camps were opening everywhere. Claude Perkins
ran buses to the shipyards every day. The benevolent credit system
that had kept so many families alive during the desperate Depression was coming to a close.

This photo was taken in 1967 of the Zimmerman Grain Company grain elevator built in 1916.

My father and Eddie were excellent bill collectors. They took animals in trade for old debts, giving liberal value to clear the books. I remember feeding these underweight animals. There was now enough money to build the first section of a new feed store and office on land long owned by my family; right behind the bank building. Soon the feed milling equipment was moved here from the elevator to make room for the seed cleaning machinery at that location. The expansion at that time proved to be very wise.

Shortly after we moved into the new building, a distinguished looking gentleman came into the office with Mr. Brewster of Hodsen-Brewster Milling Company of Portland and advised us he wanted to grow a few turkeys. This had to be the biggest understatement of all time. Later we found out that this likeable, quiet, unassuming man had been given a million dollars on his twenty-first birthday by his father, lumber baron L B. Menefee. His older brother received the same gift. They advised they would be ready to start receiving feed at several locations on the ranch they had just purchased on Turner Creek Road, eight miles west of Yamhill. His name was Pluner Luther Menefee. One surely can see why he went only by the name P. L. Menefee.

The man is P. L. Menefee. He was by far Zimmerman Grain Company's largest customer until the company moved to Modesto, California in the 1960s.

Gordon Zimmerman Photo

P. L. Menefee's home at his A Ranch on Turner Creek Road eight miles west of Yamhill. The house was built in 1946.

Mr. Menefee and his wife soon had a house designed by Pietro Belluschi, one of the most famous architects in the country, under construction on a knoll overlooking this valley facing toward Yamhill. The main hatchery building, brooder sheds, and homes for workers were also soon under construction, along with fenced range and feed storage areas.

By the spring of 1942, Menefee Turkey Ranch and Zimmerman Grain were expanding all over the countryside. War rationing for lumber, new trucks, gas and tires were of no concern to us. We had the highest rating available for all scarce materials the same as shipyards. It seems that the Department of Agriculture and the War Production Board became aware that turkeys put on more pounds of edible protein per pound of feed consumed and man-hours of labor to grow than any other farmyard animal. Also, they realized that production could be increased very rapidly. Soon, the army put out a call for all the turkeys that could be produced for use by our servicemen.

Menefee expanded all over the countryside. They soon became the largest turkey ranch in the world. Eventually, they were raising 385,000 turkeys at one time. Their brand name was: Better Broad Breasted Bronze Turkeys.

The original Turner Creek Farm was soon called A Ranch. Within just a few miles, they eventually had the B, C, D, E, F, G, & H ranches. Some were just 100 acres or so. Some were several hundred acres. Soon hundreds of men, women and children were employed. Chicken production also expanded. Soon the Carlton & Coast Railroad Station was remodeled into a chicken processing plant with freezer rooms added on each end of the building.

It did not take long for other farmers to start fixing up old barns and sheds for brooder houses and feed storage. The only limiting factor was whether a farmer could get a feed contract from one of the major feed mills in Portland for a guaranteed supply of special turkey feed. These were Albers Milling Company and Crown Mills (later to become Centennial Mills) on NW Front Street or Hodsen-Brewster on SE Second and Clay Street. Because we had been in business for so many years, we could buy from all of them. By 1943, Zimmerman Grain was supplying feed for over 600,000 turkeys. We had five trucks on the road. I was driving one of the feed trucks from Portland to the turkey farms much of the time. Also, at the beginning of the war those farms that did not grow turkeys started, or expanded, dairies because the price of milk went

Edward F. Graham Photo

Thousands of loads of turkey feed have been hauled to Yamhill from Crown Mills in Portland, here seen behind the *4449* May 12, 1975 during the Freedom Train stop at Union Station.

up high enough to make it economically feasible to start or enlarge dairy herds. One could observe all over our valley that farmers had repaired their barns and in many cases, they had erected large silos to fill with what otherwise would have been low-grade hay. Prior to WWII dairies were important but not as much as they became during the war years. Many, many tons of dairy feed went out of Zimmerman Grain and the tonnage of dairy mix made in Yamhill became a very significant part of that business.

One day I had a close call. At an Albers Milling loading chute under Broadway Bridge, sacks were coming down the chute extension towards the front of the truck where I was stacking them one at a time. When they were about half loaded, the supply stopped. I was soon advised they would not have any more for about three hours. I would have to wait. There was a large ship tied up under the Broadway Bridge. To kill time, I walked over to see if I could get on the ship and look around. I had never been on an ocean going ship before. I went on board and walked from one end to the other; still nobody around. Then I went downstairs and found what looked like a dining area. There were dirty dishes, but no people. I proceeded further down and found the hold. I thought, "Gosh! It's big and very empty." I saw one guy on his bed with his door open. I started to speak and was cut off with a, "Don't bother me. I am off duty," and slammed the door in my face with his foot. I then went to the top deck and looked over the railing at my truck. I had been gone an hour and my truck needed moving. Still nobody. After moving the truck, I went into the office to see how things were progressing. I was there for about fifteen minutes. You can guess my surprise when I went back under the bridge to see the seemingly deserted ship steaming down the river at a rapid rate. I never went snooping around ships after that experience.

All grain used was locally grown except for the dozens of cars of corn from the Midwest. In total, we shipped or received about 100 railroad cars a year. All of this feed was delivered to farmers in 100-pound sacks. Many times I put a heavy tarpaulin over the 130-sack load of feed because it had started to rain. My ever present thought while traveling the last few miles to a farm was, "Please, do not let me get stuck today." I matured with a great respect, fear and hate of mud. I have that same sinking feeling today when tied up in traffic to when I would get stuck in the mud so many years ago.

Turkey expansion was going all over Yamhill County with several million turkeys being raised. The Yamhill county seat in McMinnville still has Turkeyrama every year even though there are no more turkeys grown in the county. During the 1960s, Holland white turkeys had been improved so they had larger sections of breast meat. Formerly their breasts were very thin, compared to bronze turkeys. As soon as this new broad breasted Holland white turkey became available, it marked the end of turkey growing in Oregon. Turkeys could now be grown in hotter climates. The Menefees moved to Modesto, California, where they could now survive the heat and it was not so rainy. Almost all turkeys available in the stores today are Holland white.

Also during the early 1940s a farmer who had a barn suitable for dairy cows soon fixed up that barn and entered dairy farming or enlarged existing herds. The new Co-op Creamery in McMinnville had just opened. The demand for milk was good and the Co-op would accept all the milk that could be delivered to them. It was all in 10-gallon cans. For a time I was milking fifty-seven cows with a two-unit milking machine during the evening milkings. Another person milked the cows in the morning. I recall that we had an amazing collection of cows in differing physical conditions, many taken as payment for old bills. Most were fattened up. Some however, were sent to the stockyards in Portland if they were not soon good milk producers. The yards were where the Exposition Center now stands in North Portland.

Over the years the supplying of dairy feeds surpassed the tonnage supplied to turkey growers. The feed for turkeys was a special mix in pellet form that was made by the feed mills in Portland. The feed for dairy cows was prepared in our feed mixers in Yamhill. It was hauled to the farms mainly by the individual dairymen in 100 pound sacks. After the war dairy feed soon surpassed turkey feed in tonnage from our Yamhill plant. The days the milk checks would arrive in the mail would be looked forward to by all-producers and creditors alike.

There was another crop that became extremely important to Yamhill all during the 1940s. This was the growing of Austrian field peas and Common and Hairy Vetch. In the late 1930s, before the days of commercial fertilizer, it had been found that the growing of this legume as a cover crop between cotton rows, greatly improved cotton production in the South. Here again, the USDA and the War Production Board requested farmers in the Willamette Valley to grow these crops as it so greatly improved the yield of cotton for military use. Consequently, there was no problem getting the necessary materials to clean and process this important crop. We shipped about thirty-five railroad carloads of these seeds every year. At one time, it seemed about twenty-five percent of all the boys from the high school worked at Zimmerman Grain or Farms every year.

In 1942, during the first year of World War II, the United States Army built Camp Adair Army Training Center at Wellsdale, eight miles north of Corvallis. During the construction of this camp, every piece of lumber from every sawmill within fifteen miles of Yamhill was shipped by rail south to this 70,000-man army camp.

During June, 1943, the SP station agent at Carlton informed by my dad that the railroad would be closed for four days beginning on Friday for track repair. I was running the elevator at the time. For the next several days, I got the remainder of last years grain loaded in boxcars. The last train came through on the appointed day and hour, took all our loads and left our sidings full of empty cars and two cars loaded with feed.

This ploy worked only once. That evening, a loaded 13-car troop train came by the front of our house north of Yamhill. There were troop trains through Yamhill every two hours for the next four days. For the rest of the war, every six months, there were at least fifty troop trains passing through Yamhill each time a division was shipped out of Camp Adair. Several times a year, a trainload of sailors bound for Tillamook Blimp Base at Tillamook passed through Yamhill.

Each time the army troop trains had finished, convoys of hundreds of trucks each operated north through Yamhill to Hillsboro, over Cornelius Pass to bypass Portland and on to Longview Bridge on their way to Fort Lewis. There were few breaks in these convoys that operated for about five days during the shipping out of each division.

In the late fall of 1943, I led one of these convoys. I was nearing Westside Road and Meadow Lake Road, when I could see a whole convoy coming at me. I had just made a feed delivery. At the intersection I drove my pickup across the road and waved my arms so they could not go anywhere. I was soon surrounded by troops with drawn guns. I informed them that they had missed a turn a mile back. They were on a dead-end road. After the main convoy was pointed in the right direction at Carlton, and no easy place to make a u-turn for a mile of trucks, a first lieutenant jumped in my pickup when I said I could lead them back on the Moore's Valley Road to their main route at Yamhill. The lost convoy was returned.

Later that summer, I had my induction physical. It was harvest season. I had been working eighteen to twenty hours a day. We could not get help. This had been going on for weeks. The Army sent me home. They said I may have heart trouble and that I should go see a doctor immediately. With the way I was feeling, I was not surprised. The doctors found that I must have had rheumatic fever in my early teens. It had been misdiagnosed as growing pains. At age thirteen there were days when I was doubled up with pain. My doctor said not to worry. Every time he saw me I was another inch taller.

I had been under agricultural deferment, 2C. Because I had been under this deferment, the draft board would not list me as 4F. Instead, they listed me in a special 2-CF that meant I had to stay in agricultural work. No going back to college. The Methodist minister lost a son in the war. I had lost a good friend that was a tail gunner in a B-29 that crashed. Many times around Yamhill, many people would say just behind my back so I could hear, "I see George Zimmerman is keeping his son out of the war."

The Methodist minister, who had just lost his son, let it be known that it might be easier if I did not attend his church. These were desperate times. Gold stars were going up everywhere. Within a short time I was feeling much better and returned to working an easy six to eight hours per day. One day in Portland, while getting a load of feed, I found a cane on a street. Immediately, I was treated with kindness instead of scorn. Away from Yamhill, I used it. I survived, mentally. By the next year, I was back to the old 16-hour days, six and seven days a week in season — I did my part.

Chapter 17

The Carlton & Coast Goes to War

We all know that Pearl Harbor happened on December 7, 1941. On Monday, December 8th, while everybody in the office was listening to President Roosevelt's famous speech, a United States Army general and several other high ranking officers walked into the office of Gilbert Kneiss, an assistant to the President and head of Public Relations for Western Pacific Railroad in San Francisco. They wanted to purchase all of the rail not being used and all other rail equipment they could quickly acquire for use by the military. They knew all kinds of military units would be needing rail materials. I became acquainted with Mr. Kneiss in the 1950s and he told this most remarkable story!

When he had finished advising the officers just what the Western Pacific could offer, he asked who else beside the Southern Pacific were they going to check for materials. They told him they did not know of any other home office for a railroad nearby. He told them to sit back down. Gil then proceeded to dig out files he had on short line railroads in eastern Nevada, California, Arizona, and Oregon. Most of these were not even in the official railroad guide anymore because they were private or abandoned railroads. They were former logging and mining railroads. Like land one could not even give away old railroads. These officers did not realize they were in the office of the most active, intelligent and completely committed rail fan in the western part of the United States. Besides, he was in a very high position on a busy railroad. They could not have known that he was also the chairman of the Railway & Locomotive Historical Society, Pacific Coast Chapter. He cooperated in getting them information on hundreds of miles of abandoned rail lines and pieces of equipment. He gave them a plan on how to remove the material, mostly by the Western Pacific. Gil got the Army to agree on how to save certain pieces of equipment from eastern Nevada railroads. He also persuaded them that it would be a crime to destroy certain wooden passenger cars that he knew went into back shops in 1907, when the railroads had to have air brakes installed instead of men running through cars, setting each cars' brakes by hand. He knew of preserved steam engines from the 1870s. he also advised them of short line railroads that had been abandoned in Washington and Oregon, including the burned-out Carlton & Coast.

By the time the officers had left that afternoon, they were flabbergasted. One even mentioned, "Maybe we are going to win this war." Thousands of pieces of equipment, cars loaded with rail spikes and tie plates and rail that were immediately re-usable went directly into the war effort. There were hundreds of miles of abandoned rail lines in eastern Nevada, too. Through all of this, the Army kept its word. Pieces of equipment that Gil wanted to save ended up at the Western Pacific yards in Oakland. Over the years, this equipment had to be moved around due to land sales, etcetera, at great expense to the Historical Society. In 1981, this Gilbert Kneiss collection became the nucleus of the California State Railroad Museum at Sacramento, California. This is now the premier railroad museum in the United States. Because of the early awareness of the existence of the Carlton & Coast by the Army, the contract was signed and ready for Alaska Junk to start removing the railroad in early 1942. Snow was still on the ground.

The 1939, fire had roared up Fairchild's Creek destroying the twenty-six trestles, four that totaled over 1000 feet in length with some reported to be over 200 feet high, with a built in S curve. There was no way the trestles could be rebuilt. A unique plan of salvage was put together. L. H. & L. Sawmill in Carlton was doing salvage logging near the headwaters of the Trask River. They had already taken over Joe Flora's interest in the railroad. Log trucks were now going down Turner Creek, past Menefee Turkey Ranch, and through the middle of Yamhill to the mill in Carlton. It was decided that L. H. & L. would build a usable logging road down the east side of the Fairchild's Creek. It was a steep sixteen percent grade, but no steeper than that encountered in other areas of logging by truck. A one-mile road was built straight down the mountain crossing and re-crossing the loops created by the railroad. This isolated section of road was then graded and made ready for logging trucks. Next, nearby ties and rails were relaid on this road connecting the usable lower portion of the Carlton & Coast, with its long isolated upper portion that had been isolated by about six miles of loops and burned-out trestles.

Note fire devastation. Quick logging saved most of these trees. A new forest almost ready to harvest is now on this land.

Carlton Grade School Photo
Some very rare single bent trestles such as this were up to 200 feet high.

Mel Wasson Photo
A train of logs, some logs up to 72 feet long, at log dump on Carlton Lake. There were no airbrakes on these disconnected trucks. At the top of the mountain, hand brakes on each truck were tightened by brakemen.

At this point, the fun really began, but this was nothing new to the old time loggers. They had been familiar with setting up a series of upright steam powered donkey engines. There were plenty of them still in the woods to be salvaged. They were very familiar with setting up a series of these engines and pulling logs up a forty-five degree slope to the railhead for well over 1000 feet at a time. They also set up pulleys and pulled logs down the mountain in a very controlled manner to the railroad. Consequently, it was easy for these guys to set up a series of donkeys along the side of the new rail line. Then, the engines and cars were pushed one by one over the edge to the new sixteen per cent grade and held back by the well-anchored donkey engine cables. Workers advised that this was a tedious, time-consuming but relatively easy job.

There were six to eight steam engines brought out of the woods and hundreds of various kinds of cars. One Sunday afternoon I was looking around the C & C yard in Carlton. I ran across their passenger cars. I knew I had seen them before. It was 1939 on a Sunday afternoon and my dad and I were getting a load of hay when a passenger train was taking the loggers back up into the woods after a weekend in town. There enfolded not more that 100 feet before me,

Gary Oslund Collection

Two donkey engines, one with spar tower used to drag logs to the railroad for loading. Scraping of the C & C was during 1942.

Gary Oslund Collection

Donkey engine mounted on logs. By attaching them to a pulley and a tree stump, these ponderous machines could pull themselves up a 45-degree grade.

Gary Oslund Collection
Throughout the salvage area small fills and culverts had been washed out.
Temporary repairs were made to get the equipment out.

while driving a truck in a hay field, a picture I will forever hold in my
memory. I was sixteen years old. First was a Shay steam engine. Next,
came three or four boxcars that I assumed were camp supplies. Then
came a boxcar with openings in the side to serve as windows. After
that came two wooden passenger cars that had no windows because
they had been broken out by earlier passengers. I believe they were
built for an electric interurban line about 1910 and I was sure they
had never been painted since.

Next came two cars, each about the size of a bus with a single
axle under each end. Bringing up the rear was a trailer from a track
worker's speeder with a cable attached to the coupler at the rear of
the train, then passed through about a 2-inch steel pipe about eight
feet long. On this trailer eight men were seated back to back. One
could tell that the entire train was packed with men. I will never forget the scene. The men were to travel about thirty miles over huge
trestles in high heat to get to their logging camp. No wonder so many
of them were still drunk.

This decrepit train was a typical Joe Flora operation. It is known
that many of these men wondered if they would come out of the
woods the next weekend alive. One man was killed at a Flora camp

every week or so. He was famous for saying, "Put the body over there, boys, and get back to work. Bill, you take his place. We will send the body out on the next train tonight." It was because of this incredible slaughter of men in Flora logging camps that the Oregon State Industrial Accident Commission was founded. A former switchman once told me that Flora would send men over to railroad cars and cut off either a grab iron or a flat step whenever a short piece of metal was needed to handle logs. More than once a switchman would jump on the end of a car only to find that there was no place to hang on or stand, then fall and lose the end of a leg, only if he was lucky and not killed. It is also, because of these types of conditions, that we have federal railway inspectors today.

It was just a few short weeks after I had seen the C & C train returning men to the woods, a forest fire started at a log recovery operation at the south end of the 1933 Tillamook burn. The fire soon spread south into untouched old growth timber in the North Yamhill River Watershed. It soon roared up its Fairchild Creek tributary and destroyed the bridges on the C & C Railroad. One was reportedly the highest single bent trestle in the United States. Some claimed that it was negligence of Flora in allowing logging on a day too hot and not safe for operation and the use of primitive chain saws that caused the fire.

The fire of 1939 broke Flora. He was an extremely capable man over a period of many years. Over the years, I have heard many stories about Joe Flora's logging operation west of Yamhill. he drove his men and took chances that would never be allowed today. He had started Flora Logging Company in 1922 and became one of the largest logging operations anywhere in the Northwest. He soon purchased the controlling interest in Carlton & Coast Railroad.

The original 1910 line extended to Tillamook Gate which was located only about three miles north and west of the present day Flying M Ranch.

From Fairchilds on, the railroad had been built as a private logging carrier. In the *Official Railway Guide* in 1938, it was shown as ending at Tillamook Gate even though the last three miles had been torn up, for many years. Private railroads did not have to report anything in the ICC. A typical logging railroad had been built up Hannah Creek to the summit of the Coast Range where they built Camp One. Four per cent grades or steeper were used. The line was known as the Flora Logging and Carlton & Coast Railroads

The new lodge at Flying M Ranch, 2003.

at different times. Over the years, the railroad built about seventy-seven miles of track. Much of this was spurs built into a new area to log one year, log the next year and then move the line to a new location to be logged the next year or two. One of the longer spurs was one built about 400 feet up along the side of the mountain along the north side of Meadow Lake. Here logs were pulled up to the railroad by huge steam donkeys or pulled down to the railroad right-of-way by the same donkeys during the 1920s.

Over the years the Carlton Lake sawmills were plagued by fire. However, they were re-built and the C & C would supply logs to all of them. There was also a Southern Pacific Railroad spur down what is now the west end of Monroe Street in Carlton at what was a log loading area at the east end of the dam across the North Yamhill River. Here train loads of logs were sorted, cut to proper lengths and loaded. They were shipped by SP to a point on the Willamette River in South Milwaukie named Menefee, named after P. L. Menefee's father L. B. (Lucious Bachtavious) Menefee. After the logs were placed in the river, rafts were formed and the logs were floated to Weyerhaeuser

	25 Motor.	M ls	*February*, 1931.	22 Motor.		
			LEAVE] [ARRIVE			
	†11 30 A M	0	........**Carlton**.......	9 00 A M		
	11 33 ″	1	.........Johnson.........	8 56 ″		
	11 53 A M	5.2	.........Woods.........	8 36 ″		
	12 01 P M	7.3	...........Pike.........	8 28 ″		
	12 15 ″	10.7	......Cedar Creek......	8 15 ″		
	12 20 ″	12.0	........Fairchilds.......	8 10 ″		
	12 22 ″	12.1	......Chesterbrook.....	8 08 ″		
	12 30 P M	14.1	...**Tillamook Gate**...	†8 00 A M		
			ARRIVE] [LEAVE			

CARLTON & COAST RAILROAD COMPANY.

J. C. FLORA, President,   Carlton, Ore.

ED. KINGSLEY, First Vice-President.   Portland, Ore.

GEO. L. GARDNER. Second Vice-President,   ″

THOS. RICHARDSON, Secretary,   Carlton, Ore.

Trains marked † run daily except Sunday.

STANDARD—*Pacific time.*

Connection.—At Carlton—With Southern Pacific Co.

Gordon Zimmerman Collection

A February, 1931 listing of the Carlton & Coast Railroad in the *Official Guide of the Railways.* All thought of building on to the coast was abandoned when the line reached Fairchilds and a switchback was installed.

Mill in Longview, Washington. Because of the very steep grade out of the Carlton loading area, only a few cars at a time could be brought up the hill to the main line siding in Carlton. A train load of logs would be shipped to Menefee every few days.

The Reconstruction Finance Corporation granted Flora Logging Company a loan in 1932 to move the main line from the four plus percent grade of their original main line up Hannah Creek to a new line already started in 1929 up Fairchild's Creek with it's huge trestles mentioned earlier. The new line left the old 1910 line about a mile east of the Flying M Ranch at Fairdale and extended for twenty-one miles through very heavy timber lands to a point called Cody near the Coast Range summit on an extension of the original Hannah Creek line. This gave access to thousands of acres of timber. Even though times were hard during the 1930s, some logging was accomplished and the C & C still delivered up to 100 carloads per day of logs to Carlton Lake all during this time.

Photo by Clarence B. Mitchell 1885 – 1971
Courtesy of his children – Bryce G. Mitchell & Eleanor B. Mitchell
Flying M Ranch, Yamhill, Oregon

This picture was taken in the late 1920s of a single switchback on the Carlton & Coast Railroad at Hannah Creek Tributary to the North Yamhill River at Fairchilds. Today this site can be reached by a ½ mile trail from the Flying M Ranch Campground. The main line track takes off up the hill beginning behind the third car from the left. The disconnected log cars are coupled together on the trestle across the bottom of the picture, which served as the trail track for the single switchback at this location. Here, the Shay geared type of steam engine has just come down off the high line and is now pushing its load of logs to a rod type of engine for hauling to the mill in Carlton. The Shay will then back up to an oil loading spout below the large oil tank on the hillside on the extreme right hand side of the picture. The Shay will then fill up its tender with oil that had been delivered by tank car to the siding on the upper main line above the eighth log car from the left. Here, oil was fed by gravity from the tank car through a pipe on a trestle to the left of the top of the oil tank. After the Shay was filled with oil, it would return to the water tank fill up, connect itself to the flats and return to a logging camp for another load of logs. Only the weight of the logs sitting on these disconnected flats kept the train from pulling apart. Notice the flat under each end of each load in the middle of the picture. This system worked as the grades were all downhill. This line was replaced in 1932 by the new line that went up Fairchild Creek. Its four huge trestles were burned in the great fire of 1939.

Tom Ballard, News Register *Photo*
Former Carlton & Coast #5, now Mt. Rainier Scenic Railroad #5 at Elbe,
Washington. Picture was taken at McMinnville, Oregon during 1989. Used for the
filming of movie, *Come See the Paradise*, at McCoy, south of Amity.

After the 1939 fire, Joe Flora declared bankruptcy, moved to
northern California, and started a new logging company. In 1946
he committed suicide. During the 1930s, the Flora Logging Company offices were upstairs in the Yamhill State Bank building. By
late 1939, the Reconstruction Finance Corporation had removed
all Flora Company records from this building which is now owned
by the author.

By 1943 all of the Carlton & Coast had gone to war. All of the
steam engines went to other logging railroads except one that went
to the Port of Vancouver. One of their engines has survived. It is
number five and operates on the Mt. Rainier Scenic Railroad at
Elbe, Washington. I was the caretaker for cars used with this engine
in the filming of the movie, *Come See the Paradise*. We traveled from
Portland, through McMinnville in 1989 to McCoy south of that city.

All of the equipment removed was in typical Flora disrepair
and was rebuilt or scrapped. Some of the disconnected flats were
shipped to other logging operations in the area. While loading cars
of grain at Yamhill, flat cars loaded with railroad wheels and axles,
other railroad equipment and carloads of scrap were often seen
going north on our daily Hillsboro turn.

1917 — Near Dee

The Carlton & Coast Depot at Monroe & Kutch Streets. The building is covered with sheet metal since its use during World War II as a chicken processing plant.

L. H. & L. Lumber Company soon opened a one way road for trucks on the railroad right of way. The trucks returned to the camps using Pike and Turner Creek Roads. Heavy logging started in the new fire area as well as the 1933 burn area. C. F. (Sport) Laughlin was L. H.& L.'s primary logger. Most of the logs were salvaged during the next ten years before insects and rot made the logs worthless. By today's standards logging in the 1930s and the 1940s was still very primitive. There were some gasoline-powered chain saws, but they were very heavy and hard to use. Many took two men to operate. They were always breaking down. Many started forest fires. The men worked under extremely spartan conditions. Cutting a spar or anchor tree was very difficult and time-consuming. One man with a handsaw and with pole climbing spikes on his legs would throw a rope around a tree. He worked his way up, cutting limbs as he climbed. These were extremely primitive conditions. If after and hour or more, it was necessary to use the bathroom, pants were lowered and the mission was accomplished. Whenever I see a port-a-potty on a small trailer at a job site, I think about the problem of early day loggers high in swaying trees.

Logging in the 1939 fire area continued until the 1950s. The burned logs were salvaged. There is now a new forest almost ready to harvest from this area of such devastation and early hardships. If managed right, it can be a continuing asset for the Yamhill area for now and future generations.

All during the 1940s and the 1950s there were six or eight trains a day through Yamhill. The only one that stopped was the St. Joe Turn that operated six days a week from Hillsboro and St. Joe, two miles north of McMinnville. It served thirteen sawmills and seven grain elevators. Throughout the war years there was always a problem of getting enough railroad cars to ship grain to the Portland terminal grain elevators. There were times that no grain could be received because all grain bins were full and trucks would be waiting while cars were being loaded. I had always been friendly to the train crew and had our cars loaded on time. One day something happened that greatly improved our supply of cars. A train crewmember asked if I could get him some cigarettes. This was at a time when cigarettes were in short supply and a smoker could not always purchase the brand that he preferred. The next day I supplied him with the brand requested.

Thus began the time of my buying large numbers of cigarettes. I explained to Charley Eustice of the present day T & E General Store in Yamhill the serious nature of my request and if I complied, we just might get a larger supply of railroad cars. It worked. Within a short time I was supplying cigarettes to four of the five-member train crew that included the train conductor, the most important person of the crew. Most of the time they even got the brand requested. Charley would put them in a plain paper sack in advance so other customers could not see what I was buying.

My running of cigarettes worked. From then on, we seldom had a shortage of railroad cars. The train crew even let me inspect the cars consigned to Shaw Sawmill in Yamhill. They would call me over, and if upon inspection I thought that I could make the cars so they would hold grain, they spotted it for our elevator.

One day, after I had given the conductor cigarettes, I asked him if I could ride with him to St. Joe and return. He said it would be all right if I stayed out of sight while they were switching in Carlton so the agent would not see me. The train crews had removed the backs of some of the old walk over the seats and had made beds for themselves. So I slept. The beds were possible because within days after Pearl Harbor, their caboose had been sent out for main line use and they received this baggage and passenger car that was all wood, had all of its windows intact, including the stained glass windows over each side window. All of the stained glass windows the length of the celerestory roof was in tact, too. The car was built around 1890. It's kerosene lamps along the ceiling were also still intact. There is a car like it at California State Railroad Museum in Sacramento today.

A few weeks later, the train crew let me ride with them from Yamhill to Hillsboro. Here they let me off at the west end of the railroad yards so the station agent there would not see me. From there it was a short walk over to Baseline Road where I could board Oregon Motor Stages back to Yamhill. I knew then that I had a special interest in railroads, but I had to keep these trips a secret as the train crew asked me never to tell anyone that they had given me rides on their train. Southern Pacific would not have approved. Years later, Signa Belt, who worked with my mother when I was four and five years old, advised me that she always had to be sure that I was fully clothed on warm summer days whenever it was time for red electric trains to pass. It seems that I would run outside to see the trains go by the Krono station in front of our house whether any clothes were on or not. It appears that my affinity for trains developed at a very early age.

Chapter 18

The War Is Over
Ring the Bells

At the conclusion of World War II many changes occurred around Yamhill. A very big change was the end of the dried prune market. When Russia dropped the Iron Curtain separating Eastern European markets from the West, farmers immediately started to remove trees. The prune was finished. Austrian field peas, hairy and common vetch for use in cotton rows in the South were planted on much of the land, rotating with Hennison 2-row barley used for malting in beer.

Within a short time after the war, several merchants wanted to leave the area. It was at this time my father purchased their buildings. He had great faith in Yamhill. He fixed up one of the buildings and rented it as a restaurant. The building next door was rented as a lumberyard. Both were rented to returning servicemen. Soon, the new owners of Yamhill State Bank wanted to build a new building on the site of the original feed store. A deal was made, and after standing vacant for many years, my father remodeled the building into four business units. Soon, the barbershop moved into the bank's conference room unit and has been there ever since. As other local businessmen wanted to move on to other areas, my father purchased more vacant store buildings, garages, and rundown houses. Local wags soon started to call the town "Zimmermanville." All of these buildings have been repaired and sold over a period of years, or torn down if the buildings were too far gone to repair. We kept the old bank building.

During 1949, a new grade school building was built in Yamhill. When the old school building was torn down, the bell was saved and used in Yamhill's annual event, Derby Day and its parade down

Gordon Zimmerman Photo

Alexander Fryer's granddaughter, Beulah is here seen as Grand Marshal of the 1998 Derby Day parade heading to Beulah Park named after her when she was five years old.

Gordon Zimmerman Photo

Two soap box derby cars at Beulah Park, July 1998.

the Main Street to Beulah Park, named after a cousin, Beulah Fryer. She is the daughter of William Fryer, mentioned earlier in this narrative. There is an interesting family connection between the Zimmerman and Fryer families' histories and the bells of Yamhill.

During the Fryer family reunions, an insight into happenings during the early part of the century was received. Most of these people had a very good insight into history and realized the value of passing this information onto younger generations.

One of the topics discussed was the burning of the home of my great-grandfather, Alexander Fryer. The farm had been purchased a short time before by his daughter, Orpha and her husband, Charles Swingle. Willie Little, a local carpenter, was remodeling this house during November of 1918. Years later he recalled that he had lost all his tools in that fire. He had been working at this house when he heard all the church bells ringing and knew the war was over. He remembered that he threw down his tools and went downtown to celebrate.

At dusk that evening, smoke was seen coming out of the front parlor fireplace chimney. Willie had been working in that room. Soon the Fryers who lived just west across the road saw a red glow in the windows. Nothing was saved. It is believed a hobo from the railroad read the secret sign that food was given for work at this home, found the open, and vacant, house with scrap wood Willie had been using next to the fireplace. It is believed that he started a fire at dusk with nearby short pieces of wood and then longer pieces later. It is believed that he warmed up on this wet and rainy day and went to sleep. The fire would have burned out beyond the hearth, gave him a hot foot and he fled. A search was made and no body was found.

In those times, large cities would publish an extra paper whenever there was a major event. How did small towns such as Yamhill receive news? By the Sunday before the Armistice it had been published in newspapers that an armistice would soon be signed. This was such major news that most churches in each community followed suggestions in the newspapers to ring all bells when word finally came that an Armistice was about to be signed.

As soon as it was known that the Armistice would soon happen, how did word get to small towns in this time of no phones or radio? All major railroad headquarters would have received word by newspapers or telegraph. This was then relayed to each and every railroad station in the United States where the news was then relayed to local churches. An aunt told me that she and others rang the bell in the Methodist Church for about an hour. Telegraph lines on all railroads were the major communication system of that time.

Willie Little would have had no trouble hearing three of the bells in Yamhill. They were from Verdun, France and are about three feet in diameter and height. My grandfather, Christian Zimmerman purchased the two bells that still remain for use in two churches

Methodist Cenn. Booklet
There were three bells from Verdum, France in Yamhill. This one is in the belfry of the Methodist Church.

that he helped organize. One bell is now in the Christian Church and one is in the Methodist Church. One of the Verdun bells also hung in the ornate belfry of the old school building. When this building was torn down, this bell was mounted on a small trailer. For many years it was used in the town's annual Derby Day Parade and in annual gatherings as Yamhill's float in all other small towns in the area. The bell and trailer were stored in a small shed behind Claude Perkins' home at Second and Laurel Streets. After a number of years, when workers went to make the bell and its trailer ready for its next use, they found it had been stolen. This was a sad loss for this small community.

In 1945, shortly before V-J Day, it was mentioned to a local minister that all the bells rang for about one hour when word was received that there would be an end to World War I. He thought it would be very fitting to ring all the bells once more in Yamhill and he made all of the arrangements. Many people realized that three, large matching bells in Yamhill were unique and could be heard for several miles. Word finally came that V-J Day was here. As soon as I

Gordon Zimmerman Photo
New Zimmerman Feed Store with its new extension of right end, near end of harvest 1947. Elevator is full; this building is full. It would be another three years before farmers brought their grain to the elevator in bulk in this area. This grain would be handled by men one sack at a time and taken to the elevator for shipping.

returned from delivering a load of feed, I ran to the Methodist Church and relieved the new elderly pastor. All the bells were ringing in town including the small Catholic bell. I rang the bell for almost an hour, the same as my aunt Ella had done one war earlier. The excitement of the moment was overwhelming. All could feel the great relief that the war was finally over. I could go back to college. It was with a great deal of pride we rang the bells of old Yamhill.

The Yamhill area has survived and prospered as land use and community needs changed over the years. Many new uses of the farmland around Yamhill would unfold in the coming years.

The George Zimmerman Farm taken about 1947. The main house with the windmill tower burned in 1950. All other buildings are now gone except the barn at the extreme left side of the picture.

Chapter 19

Yamhill
The Horse Capital of Oregon

During and after World War II many "Gypo" cut and run loggers started to operate in the area. At least 80% of the Carlton & Coast railroad grade was converted to logging roads. Most are still open today. Charles F. "Sport" Laughlin owned one of the very best logging operations, that happened to be the largest. He was a third generation resident of Yamhill living on, where else, Laughlin Road. A grandfather had received a donation land claim for his farm. This logging business is still being run by a granddaughter.

Sport was a most dynamic personality and was not afraid to speak his mind. Many years ago, there was a public meeting where someone started to complain about something that my father was advocating. I will always remember how Sport got up and in his booming voice said: "George Zimmerman is right on this matter, so knock off all this baloney and approve it and go on to the next subject." These two men knew each other for sixty years. They were of completely different types but it was so obvious that they completely respected each other and their ideas.

In 1950 my father bought a piece of land for a subdivision. He donated almost half of the land to the adjoining high school. Sport Laughlin then came in with his earth moving equipment, used in his logging operation. He then built terraces on the gently sloping existing school property and the land recently donated by my father. When the project was completed, the school had a running track, baseball field, and a football field with a large pad alongside for a stadium. This entire project was done at no cost to the school district. They are all in use today.

Celia Dromgoole Collection

Christian Zimmerman in his light buggy pulled by a trotting horse. This type of horse is on many horse farms in the area today now registered as quarter horses.

Cathy Phillips Collection

C. F. "Sport" Laughlin with Elly who was sold in 1981 for $50,000.

Sport had always had a great love for horses. His specialty was quarter show horses. By the early 1950s, he had erected a large exercise arena. This was done so he could have a controlled environment to exercise and train his horses properly every day at all times of the year. During Oregon's many rainy months, this was extremely important. Because of his success at logging, Sport had the financial resources to build a large world-class arena near his home and stables. Within a few years, he won first place in Quarter horses shows at the Pacific Grand National, the world series of rodeos held every year during October in San Francisco's Cow Palace. Sport related to me that the first time he won this honor, security guards and others, quietly came up to him advising that he should load up and leave as soon as possible after the closing ceremonies. They had heard several breeders from California and Texas that could not believe that a guy from a hick town up in Oregon, of all places, could beat out all of the established breeders. The police took the threat seriously, also. Their convoy of vehicles left San Francisco and was passed on to other jurisdictions as they proceeded north. In subsequent years he won a vast number of honors. Sport was always a winner.

Sport Laughlin's building of a large exercise arena is responsible for a whole new industry for Yamhill. Within a few years, neighbors who had a few horses would rent time to exercise their horses. Then new people to the area started buying farms around Yamhill, established stables and rented time in Sport's arena. Most eventually grew large enough to build their own arenas. Today, there are at least ten stables within two miles of Sport's exercise arena, which is located two miles east of Yamhill.

One time Sport advised that he always knew the reason he had been successful is because he found out that he could think like a horse. He knew he could out think a horse before the horse could make an unwanted move. He had told me that he had met only a few other men with this ability. A short time after he met Bob Avila, he became aware that this person also had this rare ability. He hired him on the spot. A short time later, Bob and a granddaughter were making eyes at each other. Sport knew that all his hard work would be carried forward. Bob Avila's father also had this rare talent. In just the last few years or so, Bob and Christi's son, B. J., became interested in his dad's horses. He is now winning almost everything he enters. Sport would be so very proud.

With mild winters, cool springs and summers, and covered arenas for exercising, Yamhill is an excellent place to develop horses. We have mainly quarter horses, but also Arabian, appaloosa, paint, pinto, and a few racehorses. Bob Avila, who many believe is the most outstanding horseman now in Oregon, along with a number of other sources, thinks that we can make the following truthful statement, "There is more value (not numbers) in horses in the area served by Yamhill, Oregon post office than all the rest of the state of Oregon combined." One party has even stated that we should include the first 100 miles bordering on all of the adjoining states.

Cathy Phillips Collection
C. F. "Sport" Laughlin with 15 trophy saddles and other awards for his stables taken in 1973. In 1972 Sport was charged by a bull at a remote farm. This dog, "Bingo," grabbed the bull by the nose and held on until Sport could escape. Bingo quickly became a housedog. Sport felt that he could have been killed.

Chapter 20

The Big Nestucca Road: Thirty-seven Years in the Making, Washed Away in an Hour

My father was active in many civic projects throughout his entire adult life. Within the span of my memory that began in the early 1930s, no undertaking was as dear to his heart as the building of a road down the Big Nestucca River west of Yamhill to connect with Highway 101 at Blaine. He came up with the idea of this road during his last year in office as a county commissioner. He felt that he could not afford to take any more time away from his business in 1924. He decided not to run for office again when his good friend, W. A. Allen, advised that he would carry on with all of the road construction projects that had been started if he could consult with my father on all future road projects. This arrangement was made and my father was very much "in the loop" of what was going on in relation to Yamhill County roads for years. I remember county and state road officials coming into his office and spread out construction maps for his comments. The biggest secret he withheld for years, even from me, was the survey made in the mid-1960s for the new Interstate I-5 to come down from the north near Forest Grove and follow the railroad tracks through Yamhill, and then across the tracks one-half mile south to proceed on southeast of St. Joseph. The cover story given to farmers when they were out in the middle of their fields was it was a survey for a new Highway 47. George knew that this was not true because they were spending too much time surveying for overpasses at major road crossings. They spent a week on a railroad overpass one-half mile south of Yamhill Station. For over a month, he kept track of the survey crew every day. When they were confronted on his land, he could still get nothing other than the

Highway 47 cover story. One day, these surveyors driving state and federal trucks did not come back, and the next day and next. A short time later, it was announced that I-5 would go through Portland, not over twenty miles west of that city. The site for a rock quarry on the slopes of Bald Peak that Ray Moline had shown to federal and state highway officials was to supply rock for this highway. It later became C. C. Meisel's main operation for northern Yamhill County.

The first public meeting to promote a road through the Big Nestucca Canyon was held in the fall of 1926 at the Grange hall in Beaver. There was enough interest in the project, that soon a group of men hiked about twenty-two miles from Meadow Lake west to a point upstream from Beaver and Blaine. These men were the first to find that there were no barriers in constructing a road. Groups in both counties organized to push construction. When a road district was formed, it was found that there was not enough taxable value on private land to make this feasible. It was soon pointed out that a 16-foot road with a 12-foot surface would cost more than one half the valuation of all land in the district. By 1936, the Great Depression stopped all work on the planning for the road. However, a special interest group was attempting to isolate a large tract of government timber, quietly got the road district dissolved by the state legislature.

By 1947, the subject of a road down the Big Nestucca was alive and well. I remember attending countless meetings on both sides of the mountains. McMinnville wanted the road to go down Baker Creek direct to their city. Tillamook, Yamhill, Carlton, and Newberg wanted a route that was shorter to go along the north side of Meadow Lake to Panther Creek on the east end. By 1948, my father and about sixteen supporters, made another hike of the river. All commented about the great beauty of the canyon when they reached a picnic area set up just east of the home of Bob Kautz, the leader of the Tillamook County Road Improvement District.

McMinnville had the backing of the Meadow Lake Rod & Gun Club as most of its members lived in that city. To make matters worse, the club claimed the existing county road on the lake's north side was now private. They had illegally barricaded it when a sawmill that had been operating for over twenty years near their dam closed.

Over the next number of years, the Tillamook County Road Improvement District had a primitive road built to within a mile of the west end of Meadow Lake. The Yamhill District was stopped at the east end of Meadow Lake. After having made requests to the agency for years, the Bureau of Land Management finally announced in January 1956, that they had allocated $100, 000 for a survey of the route.

After much more time had elapsed, the BLM then decided to have the road connect with a private logging road at the west end of Meadow Lake. This would make the entire road inaccessible to the public as a through road. They advised that the road would be a one way road with one way bridges with turnouts every 750 feet. It was being built so it could be closed as soon as logging interests had clearcut all available timber. My father felt that McMinnville interests had got to personnel of the BLM since they advised they wanted nothing more to do with the private club and McMinnville Water & Light Department.

My father's reaction to all of this was one of fury. He said he was going to take off the gloves and start calling people by name that opposed him. It had all been very genteel by today's standards. He got articles printed in the Oregonian and Newberg Graphic. The McMinnville papers never printed a thing about the development of this road. An article in the Yamhill-Carlton Review of July 4, 1957 stated: "To my many friends who have loyally worked with me for the development of the Big Nestucca Road between Yamhill County and Tillmook County, do not be discouraged. We have been given a setback, but not a death blow." He went on to outline the problems to be overcome. He started speaking to any group that would welcome him. He started to name names that he felt were in the background pulling strings, all from McMinnville. He started to name the lumber company that would have sole access to the east end of the road and all the vast timber stands down the river all at public expense. At meetings, numerous people came up to him and advised him that the Gun Club could not possibly have a road go anywhere near their clubhouse. Former employees and members advised him that they wanted him to know that during all kinds of hours adult entertainment was constantly furnished. This is why they were so opposed to a public road nearby.

The publicity campaign worked. After it became public knowledge that McMinnville and certain logging interests did not want the road finished as a public road, supporters were able to sit down and negotiate with the McMinnville Water and Light Department. It was true that the road would have to cross a corner of land owned by the Water Department. For over twenty years my father had been advocating a route north of Meadow Lake, then turn south just west of the summit ridge, and cross a corner of Water Department land. He knew that this route could be so constructed so all drainage would be away from the actual Haskins Creek watershed and dam. He always felt that the manager of the Water Department was taking orders from people higher up in the city.

Finally, in March of 1958, an agreement was reached. The battle of Meadow Lake was lost. The road would be built along the south side of the lake on a longer, much more crooked, steeper grades, crossing the mountain at a higher elevation. It would then stay south of the Haskins Creek Watershed and dam.

Time has a funny way of proving that some people's ideas were best after all. When a new McGuire water supply dam was built, there was no way of having this ensuing lake without a public road running along its north shore. North of Meadow Lake there would have been no road on the new watershed today.

In June, 1958, a contract was awarded for construction of 17.2 miles of road from a point eight miles east of Blaine to a junction with Meadow Lake road. A one lane paved road with passing turn-outs every 750 feet was built. This junction was the scene of a celebration marking completion of the road on Labor Day, 1961. It took four years to build through this rugged canyon even though a primitive road was available for use part of the way.

A picnic was held in Yamhill's City Park, and then a large caravan of cars drove to the junction where a plaque honoring my father was unveiled. The plaque had been purchased by his friends in Yamhill and was mounted on a stone furnished by friends from Tillamook County. The first item to be hauled over the road that was not part of the road building effort was this large stone. It had been hauled over several days before by the Tillamook Public Works Department and had been selected because its jagged top matched the top of Mount Hood as could be seen looking east from the site. The timber had been recently cut. Now that area is once again a deep forest that will soon be ready to harvest.

Shortly after this time, I was in Yamhill. I remember with what great pride my father rode with me over the completed road. However, this happiness was short lived. On November 21, 1962, just over one year later, a 40-foot dirt and log dam which formed Meadow Lake washed out during a heavy rain storm. Fortunately, it was in the middle of the afternoon. There was no loss of life, but the ensuing 15-foot wall of water destroyed all bridges across the main stem of the river and most of the road. Immediately, my father's

Bob Kautz from Tillamook County and George Zimmerman from Yamhill here dedicate a bridge on Nestucca Road. The bridge, the stone and the plaque were all washed away in the flood of 1962.

great adversary, the private, all male Meadow Lake Rod and Gun Club had filed for bankruptcy and within hours, moved everything out of their lodge and disbanded memberships. They had some of the best lawyers in McMinnville who were members. No recourse for damages was ever taken against the group. The lodge burned years later. The entire area is now a Weyerhaeuser Tree Farm. Ironically, they had been warned many times about the poor condition of their 60-year old former sawmill dam that had rotten logs for a base. Over the years, the club had simply kept adding more dirt across the top.

To the credit of BLM, they did not walk away from this project. It took several years, but the road was rebuilt, but this time as a two lane road. However, most of the time it has been a gravel road. Slowly, at a rate of just a few miles every few years, it has been paved. The last three-mile section is yet to be finally re-paved due to lawsuits from a few people living downstream who want a dead end road with little travel past their homes.

In the last few years, the BLM has eased many curves from the original road east of Blaine. Now, if one sets the speed control at thirty-five miles per hour, the speed for which the road was designed, it is a very pleasant driving experience. Increasingly, as motorists are trying to escape traffic jams on Highway 18 on Sunday afternoon, there is increasing traffic on this road at that time.

Sometime, during the late 1960s, somebody stole the plaque honoring my father. The boulder stood bare and hidden in the brush for many years. Our family never replaced it, as we felt that it would just be stolen again in this remote setting. Finally, in 1987, we learned that during the late 1960s thousands of plaques all over the United States had been stolen by street people to melt down to make *objets d'art* to sell. An underground newspaper advised people how to remove brass plaques. They advised that any plaque installed before 1964, when epoxy was invented, would be easy to remove as just a mortar held it in place.

With this new information we ordered a replacement plaque with 12 3-inch threaded bolts welded to the back that would fit into holes drilled into the stone that had been filled with epoxy. The Yamhill County Road Improvement Department helped to install the plaque, remove debris from the site, re-grade, and gravel a new parking area.

On September 7, 1988, sixty-four years after this road was first proposed, we held a public re-dedication of the site. There were many people who had attended the original unveiling in 1961 at the ceremony. The new plaque now reflects the passage of time. It now reads:

George S. Zimmerman
1885 -1976
His foresight and untiring efforts beginning
in 1924 made this road possible in 1961

Gordon Zimmerman Photo
All of the ladies that were at the original Labor Day, 1961 opening and dedication of the plaque for the Nestucca Road are seen here for the unvailing of the replacement plaque on September 7, 1988. From left: Wilma Brooks, Mary Ellen Schwarzmann, Kay Schrepel, Mrs. Walter Wirth, Evelyn Enger, Hanah Stoba and Celia Dromgoole.

The building of the Nestucca Road was not the only philanthropic endeavor of George Zimmerman. At about the same time, work was started on the rebuilding of the Yamhill-Carlton Pioneer Memorial Cemetery. In a carefully planned and executed process, George and his brother Ed began by writing letters to known heirs of people buried in the cemetery. It appeared that there was a great danger at this time that the State of Oregon would declare the cemetery an abandoned cemetery and not allow any more burials at the site. This move was forwarded by many larger mortuaries to have these old cemeteries declared abandoned to improve business for the newer cemeteries owned by these mortuary interests. This was happening all over the state.

In 1961 the first articles appeared in the area newspapers appealing for funds for support of a new irreducible trust fund for cemetery maintenance. The fund had been set up specifying that interest from the money could only be used for the cemetery's maintenance. Funds were also requested for the cleaning up, removal of concrete curbs that individual families had placed around plots over the years.

The colorful history of this cemetery was revealed in the articles appearing in local papers. It is one of the oldest cemeteries in the State of Oregon. The first burial at this site was in 1852. Sara Jane Merchant, age fourteen, died in January of that year. The original cemetery was located on flatland one-quarter mile south of the present cemetery next to the now abandoned section of Yamhill-Lafayette Road. When the funeral party arrived at the newly dug grave, it was filled with water. It is reported that the girl's mother went into hysterics and started screaming, "I am not going to bury my daughter in all that water!" All present realized that this was not a site for a cemetery. William D. Clark, the child's uncle, stepped forward and donated the present site for a new cemetery and Sara was buried there the next day. Alexander Fryer purchased my century farm from Mr. Clark's estate in 1862.

The cemetery was plotted the next year. Thirteen graves that could be located were then moved to the new hilltop site. Two of these graves were Indian Clark and Indian Jim who worked for Mr. Clark and had asked to be buried in the white man's cemetery. Gravestones were erected for these men who both died in 1850.

There is an aside in this moving project. Grant Youngburg, who farmed the ground of the old cemetery site at the time of transition from horses to tractors in the mid-1930s, advised me that for the first several years after the first use of tractors, many times they had a severe problem. Because of the great weight of their tractor compared to their horses, a rear wheel would drop into a former grave. The tractor would have to be jacked up and lumber placed under the wheel to proceed. In 1853 all graves were moved that could be located. However, it is known that in pioneer times many families would bury their loved ones in the nearest cemetery that could be found, move on, and in a few years all knowledge of a grave would be lost. Little thought was given to record keeping of burial plots in those days.

The response in 1961 to Mr. Zimmerman's appeals for funds was very encouraging. He started in 1962 removing curbs, slabs, unwanted trees; hauling many truckloads of garbage that had been dumped; and removing brush that had over run everywhere. Next control stakes were driven and every monument placement was noted on maps. One quarter of the cemetery was done at a time. The stones all were moved and carefully stored. Next a road grader leveled the reconstructed area and the stones were carefully replaced. Many were given new foundations. The cemetery grounds were reseeded and there was even enough money in their maintenance fund for the yearly care of the grounds thereafter.

There are over 1400 burial sites now available at $250 per plot. The large mortuaries in the adjoining towns continue to advise clients that the Yamhill-Carlton Pioneer Cemetery and other Pioneer Cemeteries are not available for use. With continued backing, the Yamhill-Carlton Pioneer Cemetery will be a picturesque burial site for this part of Yamhill County for generations to come. The view is truly spectacular from this hilltop site.

Carlton – Yamhill Review
A garage at the author's century farm after the 1962 storm.

Chapter 21

Nobody Likes Wet Feet
New Crops on Our Hills

As has been observed previously in this narrative, many changes in agriculture occurred in and around Yamhill County during the ten years following World War II. The loss of the East European market to Russia was the death knell for the prune industry. However, a few newer orchards hung on. They received help from a most unlikely source. Remember all of the Sun Dried prune labels we affixed during the war? The Yamhill Prune Packing Plant started receiving and ever-increasing number of orders for California Sun Dried Prunes from the Prune Co-op in San Jose. They could not fill their existing orders because of all of the prune orchards that were being removed. We were only too happy to oblige. New warehouses and homes with big lawns that would require huge amounts of water were being built on this prime agricultural land in California.

By the early 1950s, Austrian field peas, common and hairy vetch were being phased out in the southern states as green manure between cotton rows. New fertilizer had been developed to replace the green manure. Clover seed demand continued to increase. It was found that this very hard to grow crop could be scratched into the soil towards the end of a Texas summer. At this time, all grass had been burned up. As soon as late torrential rains hit, the clover would grow very quickly in all that heat. A forage crop for cattle could still be utilized before winter.

All crops grown for seeds need just over a two-month period without rain to flower and go to seed. Everywhere else in the country several summer thunderstorms kill any chance of any plant flowering and going to seed. During my senior year at Oregon State in 1949, I was taking a course in economic geography. My professor, Paul

Goddard, later to become the head of the School of Business at that institution, made a statement that I have never forgotten and I have found to be very true: "Measure the total amount of rainfall that is received during the driest two-month period, adjusting the date every year for the driest portion of the year. Do this every year for thirty years in the Willamette Valley. Next throw out the figures for about five years when a storm may have moved across the area, dropping one half and inch or more of rain. After doing this, one will find that the Sahara Desert receives more rainfall during its dry season than does the Willamette Valley." This is no more than one small, rare, short thunderstorm or dew on August mornings. This points out why the Willamette Valley has now become the seed capital of North America and why in summer it is the driest spot in the world.

Grass seed has taken over from almost every other type of crop from Yamhill County to Eugene. The little packets of seed one can observe in garden supply stores are almost all grown just south of Albany. The great flood of the Midwest in 1993 brought home the importance of Oregon grass seed. During the early summer of that year, not one pound of grass seed was available anywhere in the country. As soon as the first of the new crop was cleaned, it was shipped by air to points all over the country at ten times its regular freight.

The growing of certain types of grass seed is increasing around Yamhill. The valley grows 99% of this crop in the United States. My century farm is now in grass seed. Grass has not taken over completely here as it has further south because there are other successful crops that compete for land.

One of these successful crops that was grown here even before the war, is hazelnuts — got its name changed to filberts, then five years ago officially got this name changed back to hazelnuts. By the late 1940s large areas were being planted on former prune land. Like prunes, they do not like wet feet. They are ideally suited for the area around Yamhill as they require extraordinary growing seasons. Buds start coming out in January. During the next month they are air pollinated. In the fall, the ground is rolled smooth. The nuts start falling in October. The trees are gently shaken at just the right time to bring down the rest of nuts. The nuts are sucked up from the ground by a giant vacuum cleaner. Rain does not hurt them. Some years the harvest is not completed until the middle of November.

It is known that this interesting crop was grown in China 2000 years ago. They used them for medicinal purposes. One of their uses was to grind the nuts, then burn them and add a liquid to the ash and apply to one's head to cure baldness.

In Germany they always had been known as Haselnuben or Hazelnuts. In Italy they were called Avellana for Full Beard, after Saint Filbert. Most of Europe has always called them Haselnuben. After World War II the central marketing organization tried to have the name Filberts used worldwide. They felt Filberts was a more marketable name. Most European countries, except Italy, did not go along with this change. During the 1990s the Oregon Central Marketing Board decided to change their official name back to hazelnuts. All references to Filberts are now at and end.

Turkey grows the most Hazelnuts, followed by Italy, with third place to Oregon, and with Spain having the least amount of the four leading countries. Yamhill County, plus ten miles into adjoining counties produces 99% of the Hazelnuts produced in the United States. This crop grows in cycles. During 1997, 46,000 tons were produced. The year 1998 saw 25,000 tons.

By 1954 Keith Schrepel had taken out his father's prunes and started to plant sour cherries on the family farm north of Yamhill. He soon built a processing and freezing plant on the site of Shaw's Sawmill. This site is located just east of the railroad from Yamhill Railroad Depot. During 1955, a severe freeze killed all of his English Walnuts. More sour cherries were planted on this land plus more adjoining land he purchased over the years. This is a comparatively little known fruit that we all eat and do not realize it. His company, Fruithill Farms, processes, pits and freezes the fruit in 30-pound cans. This unique fruit is sold to the makers of frozen pies other dessert producers. It is also used in jams, jellies, fruit juices and concentrates. This fruit adds a distinctive and pleasing flavor to the end product. The business is still expanding. Shipments are made all over the United States and the Orient.

Since the early 1900s, the growing nursery stock has been important to the Yamhill area. The first large nursery in the area was Carlton Nursery Company. They did a lot of national advertising in magazines. They used a large red barn on the southwest part of Carlton for their warehouse and shipping area. This barn still stands. It was built by my great, great-grandfather, Peter Smith. He received a donation land claim for the land now occupied by the City of Carlton. He is buried on West Main Street, the only grave on the grounds of a former Methodist Church, now a private residence. His daughter Elizabeth, married Alexander Fryer. She was one of twins. Indians came from miles around to look at them. Indians never had identical twins.

The Carlton Nursery was bought by Bailey Nursery of Minneapolis. They purchased the dry root portion of the business in the mid-1960s. They then purchased the Teagarden Farm on Pike Road west of Yamhill, which is now used as their Oregon headquarters and warehouse area. They now operate over six farms, one of them being formerly owned by Alexander Fryer's oldest daughter, Ella. It was located on the south slope of Alec's Butte, adjoining her brother, William Fryer's prune orchards.

In the last few years nursery stock business has been growing at an accelerated rate. Bailey's main product line is still the growing and distribution of dry root trees. New nursery operators are opening wherever there is the necessary supply of irrigation water.

There is now almost as much land used by nursery growers as there are grape vineyard operators engaged in the production of wines.

Chapter 22

Vineyards and World Class Wines Replace Old Prune Orchards

My first knowledge of grapes came at a very early age. During the 1930s when I was still very small, my mother would give me an old knife and instruct me to crawl up into the grape arbor next to the wood shed and gather a pail full of grapes to be used at the evening's family meal as dessert. I looked forward to this as the same old endless jars of canned apples, pears, peaches, prunes, or big, delicious pies or puddings my mother would make in her wood stove for dessert did not match the huge sweet white grapes from our backyard arbor. We ate only the centers. The skins were quite bitter if one would chew them. Grape juice from them was awful. My family always called them white concords. However, about ten years ago, I learned that they were actually Niagara grapes. Our grapes were planted by J. J. Burton, the person who received a donation land claim for our family farm in 1847. My father advised that this was an old plant when he was a very small boy in the late 1800s. Cuttings from this plant grow today at my home in Yamhill and at the Yamhill County Historical Society grounds in Lafayette.

It has been reported that Niagara and some other sweet, juicy table grape cuttings came west on the Oregon Trail. These were practical people and they looked upon these cuttings as a supply of food in their new home. Most of these grapes had originated in New York State and were known to be successful in being carried across the country in trying conditions, yet could be easily grown upon arrival in Oregon. It is known that Dr. John McLoughlin of Hudson's Bay Company at Fort Vancouver gave the early settlers cuttings from his vines that would have been at least twenty years old by the time Oregon Trail settlers were arriving.

Not all the early settlers brought only cuttings suitable for table grapes. By 1847, there were reports of the first vinifera varieties suitable for making wine had been planted. However, most people arriving on the Oregon Trail did not believe in the use of "spirits." However, "spirits" were around. Remember, Ewing Young had a successful distillery in the Chehalem Valley in the 1830s even with Jason Lee's objection. The first lawful registered distillery and bonded warehouse for aging in Oregon was established at Yamhill during the late 1840s. All during the late 1800s, Yamhill was a center for "non-believers." All types of "spirits" were available.

While wineries had been established earlier in southern Oregon, the first winery using vinifera grapes to be established near Yamhill was by Frank Reuter on his homestead atop David Hill a few miles west of Forest Grove. In the early 1880s, Reuter is said to have stated that this region would someday become the "Rhineland of America." His prediction is now coming true. It is reported that his Riesling wine won national awards in the early 1900s. His Wine Hill is now the home of the very active David Hill Winery located on the north edge of the Yamhill wine-growing region that extends to just south of Amity.

For many years, in our wine growing area, there have been many articles that stated that the great Burgundy wine growing region of France is approximately the same north parallel as Wine Hill west of Forest Grove. They also stated that the south border of Burgundy was about the same parallel as a point just south of Amity. Many publications have claimed that Burgundy shared our northwest marine climate. These sources continued to state both are located just a few miles from the ocean, with most of the area bordering just north of the 45th parallel. A quick look at a globe with Ken Wright, of Ken Wright Cellars, proved that all of the above claims proved to be false. While Yamhill County is indeed at the 45th parallel, Burgundy resides at the 47th parallel. It is quite clear that Burgundy, France is hundreds of miles from the ocean and has no marine influence. There are however, similarities between the regions. They have similar rainfall and very similar total heat. If one uses marine climate and parallel, you would find that Yamhill County is almost identical to the Bordeaux Region of France.

It is also interesting to note that the first person to arrive in Oregon in the present era with the intent to grow fine wine grapes was Charles Coury. He happened to purchase Frank Reuter's Wine Hill west of Forest Grove in 1965. He was the first person to have had the education and experience to found a modern winery in this area.

Mr. Coury had studied wine making at the University of California at Davis from 1961 to 1963. His master thesis was an interesting "climate-grape connection." With a background in meteorology, he completed his thesis while in France. He may have been the first to realize the importance of the similar northwest marine climates of Yamhill area and France. He knew that the cool rainy conditions would be ideal for Pinot Noir, Chardonnay and Riesling varieties. He stated that Frank Reuter's prediction made so long ago would finally come to pass.

The people to have had the greatest early influence on wine making in the Yamhill area are David and Diana Lett. Like Coury, David received a degree in viticulture and ecology at the University of California at Davis. He then spent a year in European wine regions.

Lett arrived in 1966 and purchased land on the red hills of Dundee. It was very fitting that he should plant the cuttings he had brought up from the Napa Valley to an area known as the greatest prune growing area of Yamhill County. The prune packing plant, just west of Highway 99W in downtown Dundee was the largest of the region's packing plants. Like prunes, grapes do not like wet feet.

David and Diana Lett planted the first vinifera vines in the Willamette Valley since prohibition in 1967. It was their honeymoon year that they were perched on the side of a hill of their newly purchased property planting vines from sunny California. It was a rainy year. If one is on a side hill with southern exposure, as they were situated, the rain comes at you sideways and the wind drives this rain up at you so that you and everything you touch is cold and miserable. The rain comes up under your rain hat, not down on it! But the worst of all would have been the mud. The red hills are known to produce the most miserable, slickest all around most terrible mud known to man. I know. I picked up boxes of prunes after a rainstorm on those hills. Any gravel one can haul would just disappear. However, they knew that their planting of Pinot Noir, Chardonnay, and Pinot Gris would thrive in these conditions, even though so-called experts said it could never be done.

Along with Pinot Noir, by 1970, they produced the first commercial crop of Pinot Gris to be grown in the United States. Pinot Gris is a white wine relative to Pinot Noir and has become one of Oregon's specialty grape varieties.

By 1968, Dick Erath arrived, also purchasing land on the red hills of Dundee just a few miles east of Yamhill. He also was searching for "The Holy Grail," a chance to produce the finest Pinot Noir in the world. Red Burgundy wine is Pinot Noir by its regional French name.

These three families started vineyards before 1970. They were the true pioneers of wine in Oregon. The Oregon State University Extension Service had advised all of them that grape vines for the making of wine could not be grown in Oregon. The Service had been unsuccessful, and had pulled up all of their test plots a short time before. All of their plots had been on choice, damp bottom-land good for general farming practices. They had not realized that grapes, like prunes, need dry feet. They had completely missed this connection about this crop soon to be so dominant in Yamhill and Washington counties. In the early years, the Extension Service had been very uncooperative. Also, the U of C at Davis also advised that no wine grapes would grow north of the California State Line.

By 1970, these three were joined by Richard Ponzi and David Adelsheim. Soon, all had Pinot Noir, Pinot Gris, Pinot Blanc, Riesling, Chardonnay, and several other varieties. Within a few years, they were joined by many others searching for the "Holy Grail" of Pinot Noir.

By 1970, David and Diana Lett produced their first vintage of Pinot Noir and Pinot Gris. It received acclaim from all the early vintners. Today a bottle would sell for about $425 if you could find it. Over the years they perfected their wines. The year 1975 was considered a good year. Just how good would soon be known to the world.

The Letts are unpretentious people. Their Eyrie Winery follows that line of thought. It is not a grand building high on a hill, but instead it is still to this day in a former unmarked turkey processing plant near the railroad tracks on the north side of downtown McMinnville, considered the capitol of the Yamhill wine growing region. This building housed the plant that processed most of the turkeys from the Menefee and other turkey growers from the Yamhill area during the 1940s. It was ideal for conversion to a winery requiring absolute even temperature control for aging. This building has rooms with very thick walls that had been used for cooling, then freezing of millions of turkeys.

The most miserable job known to man is the loading of turkeys into crates that went to this building. The crates would hold about eight turkeys each. As they were being loaded, the turkeys would empty their bowels and bladders into the face of the persons stuffing them head first into crates that were already on a truck. The secret was to always stand on a ladder so one's face was always higher than the turkey. Workmen wore raincoats even on hot days so they could be hosed off every few minutes. I saw this happening as turkeys were loaded onto trucks at Menefee's. The Carlton & Coast station in Carlton was converted into a chicken processing plant during World War II. Most of the original building plus additions to each end created two large cooling rooms, but left the main passenger loading area untouched. This building is now used as Ken Wright Cellars storage facility. Mr. Wright's winery has also completed a remodeling of the Carlton Southern Pacific former Red Electric Station. Fortunately, it is located just across the street from their main winery building. They have restored all of the building's original features and have converted it into one of the most interesting Wine Tasting Rooms in the Willamette Valley. What a fitting and sophisticated shift from one large industry to another. They both have had a profound effect on Yamhill County.

In 1979, the Olympics of the wines of the world were held in Paris. There were 330 wines in competition from thirty-three of the world's wine producing regions. The Letts entered a 1975 Oregon Pinot Noir from their Eyrie Vineyards that placed an unbelievable third place. Before a panel of twenty judges from England, France and America held the following year, the Letts' Pinot Noir placed second in a competition with the six top foreign Pinot Noirs from the previous year's Olympiad and Burgundies from the cellars of Robert J. Drouhin. He is considered to be the finest vintner in France. This was the first time an American Pinot Noir had successfully competed against wines from Burgundy. In France their specialty is red wine. In Yamhill County the specialty is white wines.

In 1983, a Erath Vineyard's Pinot Noir was chosen as the best Pinot Noir in the marketplace. Richard Ponzi's Pinot Noirs were listed among the 100 top most exciting wines in 1990, 1993, and 1994.

The race was on. Robert Drouhin of France kept close track of what was going on in the Yamhill area. A number of trips were made to our valley and a large number of soil samples were taken back to France.

It would be ten years before this most famous French vintner would commit to expanding in Oregon. At the time, the local press quoted him saying that this area has the potential for producing wine

Gordon Zimmerman Photo

One of the most prestigious wineries in Oregon is Bernard & Ronni Lacrute's WillaKenzie Estate. It is located on part of the former Sport Laughlin Ranch and looks over the Zimmerman Century Farm two miles north of Yamhill. Note the vineyard on ridge in background. This former timberland was purchased by Grandfather Swingle for a supply of wood for his prune dryer in 1916.

as great as any in France. At the time, good grape potential land was about $3,000 per acre. In France, if one could purchase good grape producing land, it would cost from $75,000 to $100,000 per acre, but none is available. He now has invested $10,000,000 in the Yamhill area. His Domaine Drouhin Oregon Winery is located in Carlton just south of Yamhill with vineyards near Dundee.

Where will it end? Nobody knows. Today, there are 475 growers in all of Oregon. Many are on former prune orchards. Even 420 acres of Sport Laughlin's even larger ranch is now one of the more impressive vineyards and wineries. This establishment uses only gravity, having no pumps in the building to move the wine. The grapes are unloaded on the roof, processed and the liquid flows to main

Gordon Zimmerman Photo

Elk Cove Vineyards and Winery. This is the site of Oscar Olson's former Prune Orchard north of Yamhill. Beside caring for his prunes, he sheared sheep for most North Yamhill County farmers. Beginning at about age ten one of the author's jobs was tying up the fleece of wool into bundles that had been removed from the animal by Mr. Olson.

tanks directly below. Later, the wine is dropped to the next level down for final processing. This is a system used in France and is an advantage in handling "finicky" Pinot Noir. I recently sold twenty acres hillside land my grandfather Swingle purchased about 1915 to supply wood for his prune dryer. All prune dryers used four foot pieces of fir wood. There is now a vineyard on this property. There is also a very good site for a French style hillside winery. The shift from one industry to another goes on.

The making of wine barrels from oak trees grown in Yamhill County has now begun. Some believe oak barrels grown in the same area as the wine in the barrels may be unlocking another secret of producing premium wines. This is a practice in France. Time will tell.

Gordon Zimmerman Photo

Lemelson Vineyards and Winery on Stag Hollow Road was built on Stermer's former prune orchard. Their aging room has been dug out of the hillside at the rear of the winery.

Yamhill County growers are now cultivating approximately 7,500 acres of grapes, a drop in the bottom of the world's glass. They are selling all that they can make. They are doing this without any truly impressive national advertising. Why should they spend money advertising under these conditions? It is known, that in all of Europe there is little room for expansion in a northwest marine climate near the 45th parallel. Western Australia has a very small amount of area. Consequently, a most interesting statistic screams out at anyone studying this subject. In all of California's Napa, Sonoma, and Mendocino Counties and Frances' Burgundy region combined, there is now only about 80,000 acres of vines under cultivation with very limited expansion possible in any of these areas.

Experts have been studying our area for growth as a wine producing area. These experts now state that the north part of the Willamette Valley that includes the Yamhill area, has an estimated 100,000 acres of prime vineyard sites, much more than all the rest of the world combined. The potential for growth is staggering.

For now, an ever growing number of tour buses can be seen on Highway 47 as tourists are taken to visit the various wineries. Most now have tasting rooms that compare most favorable with those in California. Many now stop for lunch or stay overnight at our famous Flying M Ranch on the banks of the North Yamhill River west of Yamhill.

Every year, the Pinot Noir celebration trade show is held in McMinnville. The cost is $825 for the three-day event. Only 600 tickets can be sold. Now thousands of people apply for these tickets a year in advance from all over the world. Tickets are allocated by lottery. Try those statistics on most other trade shows. Since 2002, sales of Pinot Gris has surpassed all other white wines in Oregon.

Two new American viticultural areas were published in the Federal Register during December 2004. They are Yamhill — Carlton and Dundee Hills. Getting published in the Federal Register legalizes new appellations, a move long sought by local growers. This recognition allows wine makers using grapes from vineyards in the viticultural area of Yamhill — Carlton to label their wine using this appellation.

Chapter 23

Transportation Policy
and the True Costs of Space

In the preceding chapters, I have attempted to outline the various endeavors that make up agricultural contributions around our home at Yamhill. I have not covered all of them. Three more that quickly come to mind is the growing of a large part of the U.S. supply of sweet corn for canning and freezing for direct human consumption. This is grown on an ever-increasing acreage on our very best bottomland near a supply of river water for irrigation. Formerly, hops had been grown on this land.

Another crop on our very poorest hill land is the growing of a large portion of the U.S. supply of Christmas trees. Some are even shipped to Asian countries. This is a good utilization of our poor soil.

A crop that has been introduced in the last few years is Meadowsweet seed. This crop is a lot like canola. It has a white flower instead of a yellow flower when it blossoms. The oil from the seed is processed and is used as a base in the manufacture of all types of perfumes. It is a small, yet interesting crop. There are many other unique crops produced in our valley.

On September 12, 1998, an event occurred that would have a far-reaching effect on all agriculture endeavors in the Yamhill area over the next twenty-five to fifty years. On that date a new light rail line opened from downtown Portland to Hillsboro, only twenty miles from Yamhill. They have utilized abandoned and little used portions of James J. Hill's Oregon Electric Railroad. Tri-Met, the governing body of the area, had done everything right with this project. They have designated all land within three-quarters of a mile of the stations to be high-density use. Many developers at first

screamed "foul." They felt that they could not sell high-density housing in a suburban area. They claimed that everybody would demand
the usual large lots with big one-story houses with big lawns and the
usual wide streets. They felt that having a light rail line station would
have absolutely no effect in helping to sell their houses. Some adjoining property owners even took Tri-Met to court. The NIMBY'S
(Not In My Backyard) were everywhere. Nike Corporation purchased, at way over market price, a large block between their present
campus and a Tri-Met station. They then advised Tri-Met and the
county that they intended to build more low buildings, running
tracks, fountains, reflecting pools, lawns, and lakes, as was done on
their adjoining campus. This land was zoned for high-density usage
long before Nike had purchased the property. When Nike protested,
they were advised to show some plans for new high rise office tow-
ers with some shops on the ground floors with office space or
housing on the upper floors. They were advised that a new billion-
dollar light rail system had a station next to their property, they
knew this when they jumped in at the last minute and purchased
the property. The same old way of building in the suburbs would
not be allowed. Critics were dumbfounded. Nike stayed. They had a
massive downturn in business and no new buildings were needed.
Nearby new small condominiums, apartments, and stores were rented
as soon as they were completed, even before the system opened.
Demanding maximum density near new public transportation systems is an important first step in saving our incredible variety of
agricultural lands in Yamhill County. This zoning concept is being
adopted in other states and it appears to be a successful policy.

MAX, Portland's light rail system, has been operating with all
trains and some parking lots jammed since day one. Anyone who
had witnessed the inaugural weekend knew this was going to happen. Over 260,000 people showed up at parties at all of the stations.
Only about 180,000 people were able to ride during this weekend
event. Many were from as far as Europe to Australia and New Zealand
attending a transportation conference. Many from the convention
could not squeeze aboard the jam-packed trains. At a meeting of
this conference, Gordon Linton, administrator of the Federal Transit Administration in Washington, D.C., was most specific in pointing
to Portland as a model for other communities and for Congress and
the White House in formulating new transportation policies. These
new policies will lean heavily on what Portland has been doing to

Gordon Zimmerman Photo
The *4449* at Hillsboro next to the western end of the line for Portland's light rail trains, just 20 miles from Yamhill. Photo, July 04, 2002.

use transit to contain and shape growth. They will show the region's huge citizen involvement in land use planning and transportation decisions. It is hoped that these new policies will properly use urban growth boundaries and urban renewal. The temptation will be great to accommodate the existing land ownerships of housing developers with connections at City Hall instead of following available rail corridors, that could be used for high-density development.

Yamhill is just twenty miles and less than thirty minutes from Hillsboro, the present end of track. If, within a few years, this line is extended to Forest Grove on the Oregon Electric, a right of way that the state already owns, Yamhill will be only fifteen miles from the end of the track. The possibility of urban sprawl reaching Yamhill in about twenty-five years is frightening. This could wipe out our entire agricultural base. We have lots of drinking water from the nearby Coast Range of mountains. It can happen here. It has happened elsewhere in outstanding agricultural areas.

In the fall of 1949, I purchased a new convertible automobile. I talked my father and mother into letting me drive them to Santa Ana, California to see a beloved cousin, driving down the coast route all the way. After a few days, he advised that he would like to make the trip. For years, he had been president of the Yamhill Cooperative Prune Growers Association. He would make the trip, if we could stop and see his counterpart at the Santa Clara Valley Co-operative Prune Growers.

During the time we visited with this man, then in his late sixties, a conversation occurred that I have now remembered for two-thirds of my lifetime. This distinguished looking businessman, whose name has been lost to my memory, and my father, discussed the general decline of the prune industry in the Santa Clara Valley. They had been in contact for years, but this was the first time that they had met. This gentleman held lots of orders for prunes. This most imposing gentleman was very upset. A large grower had sold his land for a housing development. The new owner came in just days before the prunes were ready to be harvested and, against the terms of the sales contract, had removed the trees laden with a bumper crop. More orchards were scheduled for sale before the next harvest. The man understood the plight of the farmers with millions of dollars being offered for their lands. This did not lessen his distress.

There was more discussion on how every bit of Santa Clara Valley was now in danger of being "developed," as impossible as that seemed at that time. I will never forget how he stated that developers were not only taking good prune agricultural land, but they were wasting and raping it with residential buildings with huge lawns and even grander commercial buildings with even more extensive lawns that he called "Monuments to the egos of chief executives." All this meant that the units per acre were very small. He complained that they were using up all of the valley's precious water supply for lawns. At this rate, he stated, that within a few years there would be no more agricultural activity of any kind in this extremely fertile valley that could grow anything required for direct human consumption. He grew ever more agitated. He went on to say, pounding his open hand on his desk at each word, "**Mark my word, George Zimmerman, 1000 years from now, when the world is starving and there is not enough good agricultural land to produce food for the world's starving millions, in some old library somebody will find what had been grown in the Santa Clara Valley. Because the good soil is so deep, they will find that they can tear down most of the buildings in this entire valley, and dump them all in the San Francisco Bay. They could then restore one of the greatest agricultural areas in the world. This whole civilization could be shaved off because of the very deep soil in the area.**"

His thoughts were so far fetched at the time that we all just laughed. But, the way things are going now, I am beginning to believe that he may possibly have been right in his line of thinking so long ago. Someday this could come to pass in our great valley and other great valleys throughout the land that have suffered the most severe blight ever to descend unto our agricultural lands — URBAN SPRAWL.

When setting out to write about any topic, one might ask, "Where is the beginning?" Many believe that urban sprawl had its beginning when Henry Ford rolled out the first automobile that a large portion of our population could afford. They may be right. However, for this story let us say it began when Highway 47 opened in 1921 through our valley at Yamhill with a road that all just knew would be adequate for all time. My father had recently been elected as county commissioner. He ran on a platform that something must be done about the county roads. He won on a margin of twenty-eight to one, a rather lopsided-election. He was soon besieged with people wanting new level and straight roads, not trails, over every hill in sight. He did a good job. More new roads were built in Yamhill County in the next ten years than anytime before or since.

By 1931, both the Red Electric and Oregon Electric trains had been discontinued through the Willamette Valley. However, it was not to be until 1946 that true urban sprawl was underway.

Many say that Levittown, New York, started in 1946, was the first large subdivision to be placed on agricultural lands. Automobiles were again available, some for under $1,000. Like most to follow, it was beyond any established streetcar or bus line from any nearby town. One needed a car to live there. Soon, subdivisions were built in every city in the land. Some were built around freeway right of ways completed within a few years. In constructing many freeways and subdivisions, little used railroads were purchased in lieu of building overpasses. The rights of way were paved over with these new freeways or the land was incorporated in the subdivision plotting. In a short period of time, any new freeways built were soon filled with cars and trucks. The furthest thing in anybody's mind was that these railroad right of ways would be needed in only twenty-five years when the freeways, that were built to last for all time, were jammed and the right of ways could be used to alleviate freeway congestion. At the time, it truly was a new "free way" to travel.

Gas taxes only paid a very small part of the true costs of these new roads. At times, nobody thought about the huge amount of land that was taken off the tax rolls, the tearing up of many city centers and the consequences of this action. What an exhilarating experience to drive these new freeways for one who had routinely spent six to eight hours driving 200 miles from Portland to Seattle for years on two lane roads, using every secret bypass road around traffic that one could find.

It had been amply reported that during this period, manufacturers of automobiles, tires, oil, and related products formed National City Lines to purchase and then junk street railway systems throughout all parts of the country. They converted these systems using their own buses, tires, and motor fuel. What is not generally realized is that for ten years before, they set out to purchase street railway systems, and set out to influence public policies that strongly favored automobiles over city streetcars and commuter rail. For years in most cities, all privately owned streetcars were forced to maintain the complete street that they used along with other expenses, such as snow removal.

When National City Lines purchased the streetcar systems of various cities, they made sure that the cities paid for removing the abandoned rails from the streets. In many cities, they gave or sold right of ways to cities and adjoining property owners. All of their private rights of way were dispersed. This was done to make it almost impossible to reopen most of these right of ways for railroad use and to save on their property taxes, hindering any rebuilding of a railroad line.

National City Lines operated their new bus lines with courtesy and efficiency in most cities. They knew they had time on their side. They were aware that their buses would wear out in ten or twelve years. When the buses were about ready for replacement, they embarked on a program of poor service. National City Lines would then propose a deal that most cities could not refuse. They would then supply the city with another round of new buses at a fair price and the city could take over the entire bus system.

Thus, it came to pass that most cities ended up with their bus systems. However, the conspiracy still was not over as most people think. In most towns, shortly after the city had taken over the bus system, a major advertising campaign would be launched. They would have advertised excessively, "Have your own personal transportation. You can afford it!" "See the USA in your Chevrolet," and "It does not cost much to own a car. You can afford it." Personal transportation had won out in our large, bountiful land. It was only now evident to some that the great conspiracy was not to sell buses, but to lay groundwork for everyone to purchase their own cars!

However, it must be pointed out that the new "freeways" to travel were such an exhilarating experience now to drive through an area known to the driver at sixty miles per hour. Soon every city in the land wanted these new "freeways" that hardly cost them anything! The government paid for almost all of the cost. It must be emphasized that in the prevailing mental attitude, cities that had not been involved with National City lines were also soon abandoning their street cars and commuter trains.

It took twenty years to complete the interstates. Many went through the downtown core of some cities. In many cities where this happened the interstates killed the entire downtown core leaving no viable downtown section today. Only suburbs surround this destroyed core. Mercifully, for our region, the freeway passed through Portland's east side, not through the west side core. Politics kept the freeway from passing twenty miles west of Portland and south through Cove Orchard Gap.

Thus, the stage was set for the sub-urbanization of every city in the country. As jobs moved away from the central cities, a car became an absolute necessity to hold a job. With a car, people searched and found even better jobs that often entailed even longer commutes. Gas was cheap. If one did not have a car, a job in the inner city was the only one available because there was some sort of bus service there. Commutes became longer and longer and the inner city ghetto became prominent. By the 1960s, race riots started and the flight to the suburbs on the new freeways increased at a very rapid rate. Suburbs grew in relation to the freeways. Houses were not built to any grand plan. It would just make the houses fit on a piece of farmland that a developer had recently been able to purchase. It was a case of making the streets fit as they headed to the nearest freeway ramps. Anyone who would even dare to mention that provisions should be made for alternate transportation like saving or making space for a rail line to use when the freeways were filled to capacity would have been declared insane or nuts and laughed out of the room. Besides, they knew that all railroads were old fashioned and would all be out of business in just a few years.

However, by the mid-1990s the railroads are handling more tonnage than ever in their history in less time. Still the cancerous growth evenly surrounding all of our cities is expanding at an ever-increasing rate.

Although our population of cars has been greatly increasing since 1965, because of federally imposed Corporate Automobile Fuel Efficiency (CAFE) standards, cars have become smaller and more efficient. They now can travel on many more miles per gallon of gasoline. Because of this change, in adjusting dollars, fuel tax, and license fees have decreased rapidly with inflation. This shortfall in highway operating funds is still being filled by increased state, county, and city property taxes. This huge increase to support automobiles at a time of declining gas taxes is one of the major reasons the Howard Jarvis Proposition 13 initiative so easily passed in California. At this time, the sudden increase of local taxes was due mainly to increased demands for the rapidly expanding automotive use. The fuel tax going to cities and counties was only a very small portion of what was needed for highway operations. It is estimated by many experts that the fuel tax must be raised by over $.50 per gallon to cover at least a larger part of the costs associated with automobiles and trucks on our highways. The fuel tax collected could only be used on our highways. Cities and counties now provide 100% of the costs of such things as traffic signals, traffic engineering services, police and fire protection for motorists, traffic and auto theft control, street lighting, street repair and maintenance, flood control, parking facilities, paramedics, courts, hospitals, air pollution control, highway patrol, and many other related services. Yet there are many people who still feel that automobiles and trucks pay for all expenses associated with their operation. Nothing could be further from the truth.

Another expense not mentioned above is the costs of space, of land taken over now under parking and highways with subsequent loss of property taxes. I have never seen data published that will show the cubic feet of space that is needed to travel by automobile compared to traveling by train. A person sitting while riding on a train going down the tracks in new double-decker cars. This is the cubic feet of space that would be a little less than half of a single level car or about thirty cubic feet of rolling space to get one person to his destination riding a train.

Statistics show that an average of 1.2 people travel in an automobile during commute hours. One car takes up a space fourteen feet wide by seventeen feet in length, this equals 238 square feet. A car traveling fifty-five miles per hour needs one car length for every ten mph. This equals a total of 1,547 square feet which equals 23,205 cubic feet of space while traveling down the road. One car used for commuting uses this space twice a day. With ever increasing commute distances due to high close in land costs for new homes, is it any wonder our freeways are reaching gridlock? Before we made a public policy of supporting only the automobile and discarded most existing rail systems, we as a nation should have done some simple arithmetic in figuring transportation in relation to the cubic feet of space required for the automobile.

Gordon Zimmerman Photo

During the 1980s, Arco Oil Company did Extensive testing for oil and gas through Yamhill area. These trucks traveled from the foothills west of Yamhill, then the length of Main Street and on to Newberg on Highway 240. Wires were staked down besides the roads and these trucks stopped every few hundred feet and shook the earth.

All of our over-dependence on only the auto and truck industry is creating another serious problem. All over the United States, major oil companies are leaving certain areas and trading other areas with other oil companies. Recently, Shell Oil Company left the state of Oregon. The local newspapers stated that their reason for leaving the state was that they did not have enough refinery capacity for their business in other states.

The United States is in an unbelievable predicament. We are the only large nation in the world that once had an extensive rail system of many types that was destroyed by government policy. We have been a very rich country, the leader of the world. We have so much space that we seemingly have been wasteful with this space.

A few years ago, in the public press, I read about the opening of a new freeway, I-105, east and west across the southern part of Los Angeles. It crossed virgin post-WWII suburbs of homes, shopping centers, and industrial buildings. Before it was done, it cost over 1.2 billion dollars a mile. The U.S. Department of Transportation (DOT) at that time stated, "There will be no new freeways across urban areas anywhere in the U.S." At that time they advised any new freeway would be too disruptive of the cities and cost way too much. Consequently, expansion of our freeway system is now out of the question. Because of the cancerous, even growth of urban areas that was caused by previous freeways, the ramifications of this statement should be noted with the great alarm!

Most people still do not realize the truly desperate condition this country is in. Stop!! Let me repeat. The U.S. Government stated: "There will be no new freeways!" There will be only little bits and pieces constructed. What will this mean to you ten to fifteen years from now? We are losing most of our mobility at present. For example, most retired people never go anywhere during commute hours. Traffic would be worse if it were not for telecommuting. I pity the young people working in the downtown core areas of most of our cities today.

The biggest complaint of people living near any rail line is the noise of train whistles at crossings. There are too many deaths if whistles are not used. There is now a new crossing device that has just been invented. The Surface Transportation Board is now testing this new development before releasing it for wide use. It is called an Automatic Horn System or AHS. The cost is only about $15,000 per crossing. It consists of two horns, one pointing in each direction down the road. It is activated when the crossing gates are lowered. The sound covers only 3.8 acres instead 124 acres at 80 decibels that comes from the conventional crossing horns on train engines. No train whistle will be sounded at these crossings with the new system.

The activation of an entirely new commuter rail system on rusty branch lines to busy main lines occurred ten years ago in the area that was the cradle of the freeway, Los Angeles. During 1993, when the system opened, a very vocal press ridiculed the system of five lines converging on Union Station on completely rebuilt tracks of the various railroads. The system was sued by those demanding more buses on freeways that could not move. But a funny thing happened. People in greater numbers than the experts predicted would patronize the new Metro-Link System. It has been growing ever since at the rate of at least 15% a year. Their ever-present problem is that they need at least one new car a month so people will not have to stand for long distances. The system is in place. Only new double-decker cars are now needed to carry more people.

Gordon Zimmerman Photo
Yamhill's business district in 2003 looking south from Main & Maple Streets.

Traffic experts say 1,800 vehicles per hour use a freeway lane under extremely congested conditions. Back in 1996, Metro Link had lured away so many former drivers that three and one-third additional freeway lanes were created in each direction into and out of downtown Los Angeles.

There is an interesting side note here to this success story, showing how people will adapt. Even while the new Metro Link stations were under construction, weary commuters with two to four hour daily commutes were checking out homes with "For Sale" signs posted within an easy walking, bike, or car ride to one of these stations. This evidently went on very quietly which the real estate market did not realize was going on for about two years. People had had enough of long commutes. Employment agencies have reported that many people have changed their jobs to fit the trains. A personal friend who is a conductor on Metro Link has advised that in this comparatively easy job market, many people have told him that they got a transfer or a new job so they would not have to drive to work. They now ride the train. ridership is now 40,000 per day, still growing, but still only a fraction of the commuters in the L.A. area. However, it is serving as a base for further expansion. 275,000 people per day now ride one of Los Angeles County's rail lines. Ridership has grown from no rail transit to this amount in just ten years.

Because of the sins of city planners in regards to the movement of people from the 1960s to the 1990s, the only new transportation corridors we have available are abandoned, little used to heavily used main rail lines that run through most of our cities. The most prevalent type of new rail transit within our cities is the LRV's or Light Rail Vehicles. There are many new systems opened around the United States in the last fifteen years. All are exceeding ridership projections. Portland opened a system to Hillsboro, sixteen miles from downtown. It connected with their present system that extended seventeen miles east to Gresham that opened in 1987. They are now hauling 85, 000 people a day, more than projected to be using it after fifteen years. Every city that has started a new transit system of some kind has exceeded expectations.

All of the new systems are literally screaming one point very loud and clear to anyone to say that people will not abandon their cars. Given an alternative involving the same or even a little more time, people will adjust, change their ways and use a different method of transportation. This is happening all over the country involving the rich and poor of all races.

The Santa Clara Valley prune grower's president made me aware of urban sprawl and its consequences two thirds of my life ago. With urban sprawl, we are now reaping what we have been sowing for over forty years. We must condense our cities and make automobiles pay their true costs. With a light rail line within a few years only fifteen miles away, we must not let urban sprawl sweep through Cove Orchard Gap and obliterate diverse agriculture around Yamhill, as was done to Santa Clara Valley just a few short years ago.

The message is clear. Condense our cities. Encourage the Transit Village concept. Even with Oregon's stringent urban growth boundaries around every city and town in the state, we are truly in a serious crisis. Yamhill must be saved. We must provide an alternate to the automobile in all cities in our nation. It has been proven that wherever alternate transportation is available, people will adapt and use transportation other than cars. We must do this now or complete gridlock will soon arrive — even in Yamhill!

Gordon Zimmerman Photo

The last train of about 150 cars, through Yamhill during 1987. The cars had been stored for several years after the railroad had been officially abandoned during November 1984. Photo taken from the rear of the author's home. Union Pacific still owns the right of way.

Appendix

Appendix I

North Yamhill, Oregon Postoffice
Established – 1851*

Name Changed to Yamhill, Oregon – May 19, 1908

Postmaster	*Date Appointed*
Benjamin Stewart	March 14, 1851
William B. Stillwell	April 29, 1858
James M. Fryer	December 14, 1860
John W. Payne	October 8, 1869
William McConnell	August 29, 1872
Azor D. Runnells	April 12, 1878
George W. Sappington	May 17, 1881
F. Archibald	June 13, 1884
John D. Edwards	September 10, 1885
Daniel Busbee	August 3, 1887
Fred M. Sappington	June 15, 1889

Mary E. Laughlin	August 13, 1892
Harry C. Gist	May 9, 1893
Fred L. Trullinger	July 6, 1897
Oscar W. Haynes	December 16, 1912
Harry C. Gist	December 14, 1916
G. W. Brace	December 18, 1918
Charles R. Tyler	April 4, 1919
Von D. Seaton	May 1, 1936
James C. Stonebrink	July 1, 1970
William A. Layton	February 23, 1974
Patricia E. Barnes	January 31, 1976
James Duckworth	April 1, 1995
Jay Wilcox	February 1, 2000
Michael D. Le Clair	March 4, 2005

*The only record of an organization established in this area before 1851, is the Methodist Church, founded, December 4, 1849

Appendix II

McKenney's Pacific Coast Directory for 1883-84
L. M. McKenney & Company

North Yamhill on the west side branch of the SP Railroad 39 miles southwest of Portland, Oregon

Archibald, Frederick	Justice of Peace
Ball & Daniel	Lumber
Ball, William & Daniel	Steam Sawmill
Barnakf, F.	Builder & Contractor
Bedwell & Company	General Merchandise
Bennett, J. & Company	Saddlery & Harness
Brisbine, Joseph	Saloon
Busbee, D.	Stoves & Tinware
Cain, Mat	Saloon
Edwards, J. D.	Blacksmith
Haines, J. W.	Physician
Hammerschmidt, L.	Physician
Keffer, J. C.	Barber
Laughlin, R. R.	Grain Wholesale
Laughlin, Lee & Company	General Merchandise

Mesner Brothers	Livery Stable
Morgan II, H. C. & Son	Blacksmith
Perry, T. W.	Wholesale & Steam Flouring Mill
Powell, David	Bootmaker
Rice, William, B.	Wagonmaker
Roberts, A. H. & Company	Meat Market
Royal, C. J.	Hotel
Runnels, A. D.	Druggist & agent Wells Fargo
Runnels, Mrs. I. M.	Milliner & Dressmaking
Sappington, G. W.	Postmaster & Farm Implement dir
Smith, Lee	Hotel
Swenson, J. E.	Builder & Contractor
Trullinger, D. P.	Water Flouring Mill

Appendix III

Business on Maple & Olive Street — 1885 to 1902

Between A & Main

Mortuary

Hall Woodworking

J. A. McKern

T. P. Johnson Blacksmith

Meckley Feedstore

Sanders Hotel

Between Main & First

A. D. Runnels Notary Public, Druggist & Agent Wells Fargo

John Lamar Saloon

Chamberlin Hotel

Bedwell-General Merchandise

Buckingham & Fryer General Merchandise

Drugstore, Dr. Carruth

Ed Salfickey Shoe Repair

Johnson & Hutchcroft Saloon

Snider Jewelers (later Hotel Royal)

William Rude Paint Store

Between First & Second

 John Williams Livery Stable

Print Shop

Farmers & Merchant Bank

Pierce Roberts Hardware

McAllister Drugs

Quong Hop Confectionary & Laundry

Princess Theatre

Jail

Mesner Brothers Livery Stable

Non-Believers' School (Pythian Hall)

Between Second & Third

Tom Perry Woodworking Casket maker

Masonic Hall

IOOF Hall

Yamhill Telephone Company

J. D. Edwards Blacksmith

Morgan Blacksmith

Appendix IV

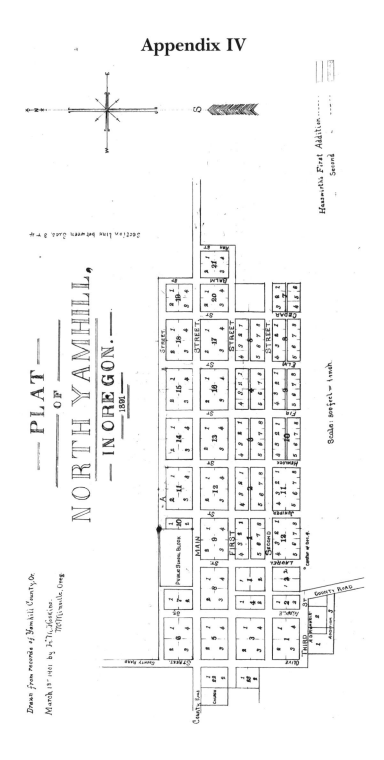

Appendix V

The Zimmerman's of Yamhill that graduated from
Oregon Agricultural College, Oregon State College
and Oregon State University 1909 — 1994

	BA or BS Degree	*Masters Degree*
Peter C. Zimmerman	1909	
George S. Zimmerman	1910	
Edward O. Zimmerman	1915	
Nona O. Zimmerman	1943	1949
Orin F. Zimmerman	1947	
Josephine Zimmerman	1947	
Gordon N. Zimmerman	1949	
Jeanette Zimmerman DeShazer	1950	
Robert DeShazer	1950	
Carolyn Zimmerman Larsen	1951	
Ben F. Larsen	1951	

	BA or BS Degree	**Masters Degree**
Martin Zimmerman	1953	1969
Dorthy B. Zimmerman	1953	
Gordon C. Dromgoole	1967	
Janet Zimmerman Duncan	1974	
Richard O. Zimmerman	1977	1978
Robert Kaspari	1980	
Kathryn Zimmerman Kaspari	1981	
Kevin C. Dromgoole	1994	

On February 21, 2003, Orin F. Zimmerman was inducted into the OSU Engineering Hall of Fame. He has endowed two scholarships for engineering and Josephine has endowed a home economics scholarship in gerentology plus funding 4-H innovative programs.

Martin Zimmerman worked for the Oregon State Extension Service from 1960 until 1989.

Gordon Zimmerman was voted by the faculty as being the graduating senior that had contributed the most to performing music during his time on campus. Consequently, he was asked to sing at graduation services of 1949.

Bibliography

Atlas of Oregon, Eugene, Oregon: University of Oregon Press, 1976.

Carlton Elementary Bicentennial Club, *Reflections of Carlton: From Pioneer to Present; the Story of Carlton, Oregon. U.S.A.:* Glass-Dahlstrom Printers and the Carlton Elementary School Bicentennial Club, 1976.

Hart, Stanley I. & Alvin L. Spivak, *The Elephant in the Bedroom: Automobile Dependence & Denial; Impacs on the Economy and Environment,* Pasadena, California: New Paradigm Books, 1993.

Lynch, Vera Martin, *Free Land For Free Men: A Story of Clackamas County.*

Palmer, Lloyd M., *Steam Towards the Sunset: The Railroads of Lincoln County.* Newport, Oregon: Lincoln County Historical Society, 1982.

Perkins, Norris H., *Slow Settles the Dust in Oregon.* Portland, Oregon: Four Mountain Porductions, 1993.

Pintarek Paul, *The Boys Up North Dick Erath and the Early Oregon Winemakers,* Portland, Oregon: Wyatt Group, 1997.

Stoller, Ruth, *From Yamhill to Tillamook by Stagecoach,* McMinnville, Oregon: Bennett & Miller Publishers for Yamhill County Historical Society, 1992.

Yamhill County Historical Society, *Old Yamhill: The Early History of Its Towns & Cities,* Lafayette, Oregon: Yamhill County Historical Society, 1976. Reprint Portland, Oregon: Binford & Mort Publishing, 2002.

Anniversary Booklet Committee, *Yamhill United Methodist Church: An Anniversary Booklet; Celebrating 100 Years In Our Sanctuary and 150 Years as a Worshipping Community*. Yamhill, Oregon: Yamhill United Methodist Church, 1998.

Rich, Nellie, "Story Told About Indians, Kit Carson's Brother Alec," *Carlton–Yamhill Review,* 9 October 1969: p.1.

Moe, Helen, "Robbery Highlights Story of Stage Travels." *Carlton–Yamhill Review,* 18 Dec. 1958: p.1.

"Home Town Hero: BJ Avila World Champion Team Roper." *CommUnity Press: The Carlton & Yamhill Newsletter,* 28 Sept. 2001: p.1.

"Ladis Kristof: The Trail to Freedom." *CommUnity Press: The Carlton & Yamhill Newsletter,* 8 Nov. 2002: p.1.

Lowe, Vincent. "Carlton's Founder Lies Near Center of Activity." *News Register,* 25 Apr. 1984: p.A4.

Lowe, Vincent. "Carlton Had Its Glory Days in Lumber." *News Register,* 28 Dec. 1987: p.A3.

Jackman, E.R. and Louis Gross. " The Settlers Prospered in a Rich and Peaceful Land." *Oregon Farmer,* 3 Mar. 1960: p.45.

Winther, Oscar Osburn. "The Roads and Transportation of Territorial Oregon." *Oregon Historical Society Quarterly,* 49: 40 – 49.

Schiermeyer, Carl H. "Metrolink: L.A.'s Cost Effective Freeway." *Passenger Train Journal,* Jul. 1996: 20–21.

Trullinger, Fred. "Remember When? How Yamhill Got Its First Electric Lights." *T-E Shopping Guide* 3, Jul. 1952.

"Those Were the Days! Adventures on Old Tillamook – Yamhill Stage Run Live Again." *The Telephone Register,* 16 February 1939: p. 4.

"Cove Orchard's Mysterious Sink Hole Still Acts Up." *Yamhill County Historical Society Newsletter,* October 1991.

Williams, George W. "The Cove Orchard Sink Hole." *Yamhill County Historical Society Newsletter,* February 1992.

White, John. "The Ghost on Alec's Butte." *Yamhill County Historical Society Newsletter,* October 1996.

White, John. "The Red Electric — Ahead of Its Time." *Yamhill County Historical Society Newsletter,* January 1997.

White, John. "The Red Electric — Ahead of Its Time." *Yamhill County Historical SocietyNewsletter,* Summer 1998.

U.S. Army Corps of Engineers. *Willamette Falls Locks.* Portland Oregon: U.S. Army Corps of Engineers Portland District. 1995.